Stories of
Repentance

© **Maktaba Dar-us-Salam, 2004**

King Fahd National Library Cataloging-in-Publication Data
Mughawiri, Muhammad Abduh
Stories of repentance. / Muhammad Abduh Mughawiri. - Riyadh, 2004
127 p.; 14x21 cm
ISBN: 9960-899-87-x
1 - Repentance - Islam   I - Title
240 dc   1425/3355

Legal Deposit no. 1425/3355
ISBN: 9960-899-87-x

Stories of Repentance

Compiled by

Muhammad Abduh Mughâwiri

Edited by

Abdul Ahad (Alig.)

DARUSSALAM
GLOBAL LEADER IN ISLAMIC BOOKS

Riyadh, Jeddah, Sharjah, Lahore
London, Houston, New York

Second Edition:Jan 2005
Printed in Lebanon

Supervised by:

ABDUL MALIK MUJAHID

Head Office:

**P.O. Box: 22743, Riyadh 11416, K.S.A. Tel: 00966-01-4033962/4043432 Fax: 4021659
E-mail: darussalam@awalnet.net.sa Website: http// www.dar-us-salam.com**

K.S.A. Darussalam Showrooms:
  Riyadh
Olaya branch: Tel 00966-1-4614483 Fax: 4644945
Malaz branch: Tel 4735220 Fax: 4735221
- Jeddah
  Tel: 00966-2-6879254 Fax: 6336270
- Al-Khobar
  Tel: 00966-3-8692900 Fax: 00966-3-8691551

U.A.E
- Darussalam, Sharjah U.A.E
  Tel: 00971-6-5632623 Fax: 5632624

PAKISTAN
- Darussalam, 36 B Lower Mall, Lahore
  Tel: 0092-42-724 0024 Fax: 7354072
- Rahman Market, Ghazni Street
  Urdu Bazar Lahore
  Tel: 0092-42-7120054 Fax: 7320703

U.S.A
- Darussalam, Houston
  P.O Box: 79194 Tx 772779
  Tel: 001-713-722 0419 Fax: 001-713-722 0431
  E-mail: sales@dar-us-salam.com
- Darussalam, New York
  572 Atlantic Ave, Brooklyn
  New York-11217, Tel: 001-718-625 5925

U.K
- Darussalam International Publications Ltd.
  226 High Street, Walthamstow,
  London E17 7JH, Tel: 0044-208 520 2666
  Mobile: 0044-794 730 6706 Fax: 0044-208 521 7645
- Darussalam International Publications Limited
  Regent Park Mosque, 146 Park Road,
  London NW8 7RG Tel: 0044-207 724 3363
- Darussalam
  398-400 Coventry Road, Small Heath
  Birmingham, B10 0UF
  Tel: 0121 77204792 Fax: 0121 772 4345
  E-mail: info@darussalamuk.com
  Web: www.darussalamuk.com

FRANCE
- Editions & Librairie Essalam
  135, Bd de Ménilmontant- 75011 Paris
  Tél: 0033-01- 43 38 19 56/ 44 83
  Fax: 0033-01- 43 57 44 31
  E-mail: essalam@essalam.com

AUSTRALIA
- ICIS: Ground Floor 165-171, Haldon St.
  Lakemba NSW 2195, Australia
  Tel: 00612 9758 4040 Fax: 9758 4030

MALAYSIA
- E&D Books SDN. BHD.-321 B 3rd Floor,
  Suria Klcc
  Kuala Lumpur City Center 50088
  Tel: 00603-21663433 Fax: 459 72032

SINGAPORE
- Muslim Converts Association of Singapore
  32 Onan Road The Galaxy Singapore- 424484
  Tel: 0065-440 6924, 348 8344 Fax: 440 6724

SRI LANKA
- Darul Kitab 6, Nimal Road, Colombo-4
  Tel: 0094-1-589 038 Fax: 0094-74 722433

KUWAIT
- Islam Presentation Committee
  Enlightenment Book Shop
  P.O. Box: 1613, Safat 13017, Kuwait
  Tel: 00965-244 7526, Fax: 240 0057

INDIA
- Islamic Dimensions
  56/58 Tandel Street (North)
  Dongri, Mumbai 4000 009, India
  Tel: 0091-22-3736875, Fax: 3730689
  E-mail:sales@IRF.net

SOUTH AFRICA
- Islamic Da`wah Movement (IDM)
  48009 Qualbert 4078 Durban,South Africa
  Tel: 0027-31-304-6883
  Fax: 0027-31-305-1292
  E-mail: idm@ion.co.za

Contents

Introduction... 9

The Mercy of Allâh.. 12

The Messenger (ﷺ) Attested to His Sincerity................ 14

The Close Link Between Repentance and Worldly
Blessings.. 16

Woe Unto You, O Dinâr... 18

Coming To Terms With The Reality Of Life.................... 22

You Have Guided Me To A Path That You Know
Not Yourselves.. 24

What I Want Is Life That Is Not Ended By Death........ 27

The True Treasure.. 29

The Accepted Repentance.. 31

Good Advice.. 32

Good Deeds Actually Remove Evil Deeds...................... 33

The Grave Of A Righteous Man....................................... 35

Mercy And Forgiveness For The One Who Repents..... 37

Everything That Is Going To Happen Is Near At
Hand... 39

Let Us Hasten To Repent.. 40

If You Really Want To Disobey Allâh...!......................... 42

The Lingering Pain Of Sinning....................................... 44

The Integrity of Fudail bin 'Iyâd (؊)................................ 46

Death Is Better Than Allâh's Punishment........................ 48

The Evil, Long-Term Effects Of Sinning... Yet There Is
Hope Until The Very End.. 50

The Noble Qur'ân... 53

A Tongue That Remains Moist With The
Remembrance Of Allâh (؊).. 55

Race Towards Repentance!... 56

The Ever-Living Never Sleeps... 57

The Reality Of Our Existence... 58

Can Even I Repent?... 60

It Was Because Of Their Repentance That They Were
Saved.. 62

The Repentance Of Ka'b bin Mâlik (؊)............................ 65

Repent Throughout The Day... 67

When I Die.. 68

The Sinner Who Constantly Repents............................... 70

Whoever Wants To Repent... 71

He (؊) Brought Me To Them So That I Can Reform
My Character... 71

Old Age.. 73

The Hallmarks Of A Sincere Repentance........................ 74

My Lord, Here Is My Forelock In Your Hand.............. 74

Constantly Sinning And Constantly Repenting.............. 76

The Advice Of Khidr (؊)... 78

The Advice Of Al-Hasan.. 79

The Covering Of Sins.. 80

A Similar Text To The Last One..................................... 81

You Have Indeed Been Forgiven 82

A Similar Text To The Previous One 83

Important Points Concerning Repentance That We
Must Understand 85

Repentance Is Sweet 87

It Is Indeed You Who Are The Rider, And I Who
Am The Foot-Traveler 89

Then How Will You Withstand The Fire Of The
Hereafter! 91

O Wretched Man! 92

By Allâh, I Will Leap Up On Them In Paradise 94

Safety...Safety! 97

Silah 98

How Wuhaib Repented 99

The Blessing Of Repentance... Or The Blessing Of
Richness 100

A Visit To The Graveyard 102

The Repentance Of Nûh (Noah) (ﷺ) 103

A Heavy Burden 104

The Ranking Of A Person Who Repents 105

An Effective, Though Difficult, Way Of Fighting Off
Temptation 107

A Repentance That Involved Losing His Leg 108

The Repentance Of Barkh 109

A Repentant Journey To The City Of The Righteous.... 111

The Thief Of The Children Of Israel 112

Be Pleased With Me 114

How To Ward Off The Evils Of Wealth 115

A Complete Transformation 116
Giving Charity To Atone For Past Sins 118
If You Have No Shame, Then Do As You Please 119
Give Charity, For Doing So Might Lead To Your
Betterment 121
How To Reach One's Destination 122
Which Of These Is More Beloved To Me? 123
True Speech 124
Allâh's Vast And Comprehensive Mercy 126

Introduction

All praise is for Allâh, Lord of all that exists. O Allâh, send prayers and salutations upon our Prophet Muhammad, his family, his companions, and all those who follow his way until the Last Day.

Allâh (ﷻ) said:

﴿قُلْ يَٰعِبَادِىَ ٱلَّذِينَ أَسْرَفُوا۟ عَلَىٰٓ أَنفُسِهِمْ لَا تَقْنَطُوا۟ مِن رَّحْمَةِ ٱللَّهِ إِنَّ ٱللَّهَ يَغْفِرُ ٱلذُّنُوبَ جَمِيعًا إِنَّهُۥ هُوَ ٱلْغَفُورُ ٱلرَّحِيمُ ٥٣﴾

"Say: 'O 'Ibâdî (My slaves) who have transgressed against themselves (by committing evil deeds and sins)! Despair not of the Mercy of Allâh, Verily Allâh forgives all sins. Truly, He is Oft-Forgiving, Most Merciful.'"[1]

Indeed, Allâh (ﷻ) has opened the door of repentance to every sinner. The Prophet (ﷺ) said:

«يَا أَيُّهَا النَّاسُ! تُوبُوا إِلَى اللهِ تَعَالَى فَإِنِّي أَتُوبُ إِلَى اللهِ تَعَالَى فِي الْيَوْمِ مِائَةَ مَرَّةٍ»

"O people, repent to Allâh (ﷻ), for indeed, I repent to Allâh (ﷻ) 100 times every day."[2]

It is truly encouraging to know that the door to repentance is always open, but what is more, Allâh (ﷻ) is actually happy when one of His slaves repents. It is important to note here that the keys to repentance are that a sinner must

---

[1] *Qur'ân* 39:53.
[2] *Muslim*: 2702.

desist from his sin, feel regret for having perpetrated it, and then make a firm resolve not to return to it.

Who among us does not sin? And who among us does all that is required of him in the religion? It is an undeniable fact that we all have shortcomings; what distinguishes some of us from the others, what raises some of us above the others, is that the successful ones among us are those who repent their sins and ask Allâh (ﷻ) to forgive them.

Sadly, some people are guilty of thinking in this manner: "Those I see around me perpetrate minor sins, while I am guilty of perpetrating major sins, so what is the use of repenting!" True, such a person does well by finding fault with his own self, yet he makes a grave, ruinous error when he loses hope, when he underestimates Allâh's Forgiveness and Mercy. To be sure, the door of repentance is open both to the perpetrator of minor sins and to the perpetrator of major sins. In regard to repentance, the following beautiful *Hadîth* should inspire hope in us all: Ibn Mas'ûd (ﷺ) narrated that the Prophet (ﷺ) said:

«للهُ أَفْرَحُ بِتَوْبَةِ عَبْدِهِ مِنْ رَجُلٍ نَزَلَ بِأَرْضٍ دَوِيَّةٍ مَهْلِكَةٍ مَعَهُ رَاحِلَتُهُ فَنَامَ وَاسْتَيْقَظَ وَقَدْ ذَهَبَتْ رَاحِلَتُهُ فَطَلَبَهَا حَتَّى إِذَا أَدْرَكَهُ الْمَوْتُ قَالَ: أَرْجِعُ إِلَى الْمَكَانِ الَّذِي ضَلَلْتُهَا فِيهِ وَأَمُوتُ، فَأَتَى مَكَانَهُ فَغَلَبَتْهُ عَيْنُهُ فَاسْتَيْقَظَ وَإِذَا رَاحِلَتُهُ عِنْدَ رَأْسِهِ فِيهَا طَعَامُهُ وَشَرَابُهُ وَزَادُهُ وَمَا يَصْلُحُهُ فَاللهُ أَشَدُّ فَرَحًا بِتَوْبَةِ عَبْدِهِ الْمُؤْمِنِ مِنْ هَذَا بِرَاحِلَتِهِ وَزَادِهِ»

"Indeed, Allâh is more happy with the repentance of His slave than a man who stops in a barren, desolate land;

*with him he has his riding animal. He then goes to sleep.
When he wakes up, (he realizes that) his mount is gone.
He searches out for it until he is on the verge of dying (for
the mount was carrying his supplies and provisions). He
then says, 'I will return to the place wherein I lost it, and I
will die there.' He went to that place, and he was then
overcome by sleep. When he woke up, his mount was
(standing) right beside his head: on it (still) was his food,
his drink, his provisions, and the things he needed. Allâh
is more happy with the repentance of his believing slave
than the aforementioned man when (he finds) his mount
and his provisions.''*[1]

This *Hadîth* clearly illustrates that no one should become
so hopeless that he refrains from repenting to Allâh (ﷻ).
In the early pages of this book, I will relate to you some
stories that illustrate the vastness of Allâh's Mercy. Glad
tidings, then, to every Muslim who constantly and
consistently hastens to repent to Allâh (ﷻ) and to ask
for His Forgiveness.

I sincerely hope that you will benefit from this book. And
I ask Allâh (ﷻ) to grant all of us knowledge, action, and
success in both abodes – the abode of this world and the
eternal abode of the Hereafter.

The author,
Muhammad Abduh Mughâwiri

---

[1] *Al-Bukhari*: 6308 and *Muslim*: 2744

The Mercy of Allâh

To all confused and hopeless souls do I present this
Hadîth, which makes clear to us the vast Mercy of Allâh
(ﷻ) and encourages us to repent to Him:

Abu Sa'id Al-Khudri (ﷺ) narrated that the Prophet (ﷺ) said:

«كَانَ فِيمَنْ قَبْلَكُمْ رَجُلٌ قَتَلَ تِسْعَةً وَتِسْعِينَ نَفْسًا، فَسَأَلَ عَنْ أَعْبَدِ
أَهْلِ الْأَرْضِ فَدُلَّ عَلَى رَاهِبٍ فَأَتَاهُ. فَقَالَ: إِنَّهُ قَتَلَ تِسْعَةً وَتِسْعِينَ
نَفْسًا فَهَلْ لَهُ مِنْ تَوْبَةٍ؟ قَالَ: لَا. فَقَتَلَهُ وَأَكْمَلَ بِهِ الْمِائَةَ، ثُمَّ سَأَلَ
عَنْ أَعْلَمِ أَهْلِ الْأَرْضِ فَدُلَّ عَلَى رَجُلٍ عَالِمٍ فَأَتَاهُ وَقَالَ لَهُ: إِنَّهُ قَدْ
قَتَلَ مِائَةَ نَفْسٍ فَهَلْ لَهُ مِنْ تَوْبَةٍ؟ قَالَ: نَعَمْ، وَمَنْ يَحُولُ بَيْنَكَ وَبَيْنَ
التَّوْبَةِ؟ انْطَلِقْ إِلَى أَرْضِ كَذَا وَكَذَا، فَإِنَّ بِهَا أُنَاسًا يَعْبُدُونَ اللهَ تَعَالَى
فَاعْبُدِ اللهَ تَعَالَى مَعَهُمْ وَلَا تَرْجِعْ إِلَى أَرْضِكَ فَإِنَّهَا أَرْضُ سَوْءٍ،
فَانْطَلَقَ حَتَّى كَانَ نَصَفَ الطَّرِيقَ أَدْرَكَهُ الْمَوْتُ، فَاخْتَصَمَتْ فِيهِ
مَلَائِكَةُ الرَّحْمَةِ وَمَلَائِكَةُ الْعَذَابِ، فَقَالَتْ مَلَائِكَةُ الرَّحْمَةِ: جَاءَنَا
تَائِبًا مُقْبِلًا بِقَلْبِهِ إِلَى اللهِ تَعَالَى، وَقَالَتْ مَلَائِكَةُ الْعَذَابِ: إِنَّهُ لَمْ
يَعْمَلْ خَيْرًا قَطُّ، فَأَتَاهُمْ مَلَكٌ فِي صُورَةِ آدَمِيٍّ فَحَكَمُوهُ بَيْنَهُمْ،
فَقَالَ: قِيسُوا مَا بَيْنَ الْأَرْضَيْنِ فَإِلَى أَيِّهِمَا كَانَ أَدْنَى فَهُوَ أَقْرَبُ لَهَا،
فَقَاسُوهُ فَوَجَدُوهُ أَدْنَى إِلَى الْأَرْضِ الَّتِي أَرَادَ فَقَبَضَتْهُ مَلَائِكَةُ
الرَّحْمَةِ»

"Among those who came before you was a man who killed

99 people. He then asked to be guided to the most prolific worshiper from the inhabitants of earth, and he was directed to a monk. He went to him and told him that he had killed 99 people, and he asked whether it was possible for him to repent. The Monk said, 'No.' The man killed him, thus making him his 100th (victim). He then asked to be directed to the most knowledgeable of earth's inhabitants, and he was guided to a scholar. He went to him and told him that he had killed 100 people, and he asked whether it was possible for him to repent. The scholar said, 'Yes, and who will stand between you and repentance. Go to such and such land, for in it dwell a people who worship Allâh (ﷻ), so go and worship Allâh (ﷻ) with them. And do not return to your land, for it is indeed a land of evil.' He left, and when he reached the halfway point of his journey, he died. The angels of Mercy and the angels of Punishment disputed with one another (in regard to his case). The angels of Mercy said, 'He came to us repentant, advancing with his heart towards Allâh (ﷻ).' But the angels of Punishment said, 'Indeed, he never performed any good deeds.' Then an angel came in the form of a human being, and both groups of angels asked him to judge between them. He said, 'Measure the distance between the two lands. Whichever land he is closer to is the land that he is closer to (in terms of being of its people). They then measured the distance and found that he was closer to the land that he was heading towards, and so it was the angels of Mercy who then took his soul.'"[1]

---

[1] *Al-Bukhari:* 3470 and *Muslim:* 2766.

The Messenger (ﷺ) Attested to His Sincerity

When one repents sincerely for one's sin, one takes the best path to achieving the pleasure of Allâh (ﷻ). The following *Hadîth* illustrates an example of a true and sincere repentance. A woman from Juhainah once came to the Messenger of Allâh (ﷺ) and confessed that she had committed adultery. She did not come simply to acknowledge her mistake; rather, she came, seeking to purify herself from her sin. She said, "O Messenger of Allâh, I have committed an offense that requires a specific punishment, so execute it upon me."

The punishment for adultery is stoning, but it is rarely applied, for it can only be applied when four witnesses see a person not just kissing or hugging someone else, but actually being engaged in the act of adultery. But this woman came herself and confessed her sin. After she was stoned to death, the Prophet (ﷺ) prayed over her. 'Umar (رضي الله عنه) said, "O Messenger of Allâh, you prayed over her despite the fact that she has committed adultery?" He (ﷺ) said:

«لَقَدْ تَابَتْ تَوْبَةً لَوْ قُسِمَتْ بَيْنَ سَبْعِينَ مِنْ أَهْلِ الْمَدِينَةِ لَوَسِعَتْهُمْ، وَهَلْ وَجَدْتَ أَفْضَلَ مِمَّنْ جَادَتْ بِنَفْسِهَا للهِ عَزَّ وَجَلَّ»

"She has indeed performed a repentance that, were it to be

*distributed among 70 people from the inhabitants of
Madinah, would have been sufficient for them all. And
have you ever found anyone that is better than a person
who generously gives her soul for Allâh (ﷻ) (the
Possessor of might and majesty)."*[1]

---------- ❖ ❖ ❖ ----------

---
[1] *Muslim*: 1696 and *At-Tirmidhi*: 1435.

The Close Link Between Repentance and Worldly Blessings

Rain had not fallen for a long time, and as a result, the crops had withered away and the livestock had died. I am referring here to a specific time in the history of the Children of Israel, during the era of Mûsa (鐴). The situation had become quite dire, and so, along with the common people, Mûsa (鐴) and 70 men from the descendents of Prophets (鐴) left the city to invoke Allâh (鐴) for rain. If one could have seen them all gathered there in the desert, I am sure that he would have witnessed quite a moving scene: people raising their hands with humility and invoking Allâh with tears flowing down their cheeks, in a prayer session that lasted for three days.

But even after three days of constant prayer, no rain fell from the sky. Mûsa (鐴) said, "O Allâh, You are the One Who says: Invoke Me, and I will answer you. I along with Your slaves have indeed invoked you, and we are in a state of need, poverty, and humiliation." Allâh (鐴) then inspired Mûsa (鐴) with the information that among them was he whose nourishment was unlawful (*Haram*), and among them was he whose tongue was constantly busy with slander and backbiting. And in so many words, Allâh (鐴) said: These deserve that I should send My anger down upon them, yet you demand mercy for them! Mûsa

(🕊️) said, "And who are they, my Lord, so that we can banish them from among ourselves?"

Allâh (🕊️), the Most Merciful of the merciful ones said:

"O Mûsa, I am not One Who exposes (those who sin). Instead, O Mûsa, let all of you repent with sincere hearts, for perhaps they will repent with you, so that I will then be generous with My Blessings upon you."

Mûsa (🕊️) then announced that everyone should gather around him. When everyone was gathered together, Mûsa (🕊️) told them what Allâh (🕊️) had revealed to him, and the sinners referred to above listened attentively to his words. They committed grave sins, yet Allâh (🕊️) protected them from exposure and shame. Their eyes swelled with tears, and they raised their hands, as did the rest of the people who were there. They said, "O our God, we have come to You, fleeing from our sins, and we have returned to Your door, seeking out (Your help); so have mercy on us, O Most Merciful of the merciful ones." They continued to repent in that manner until relief came and rain descended from the sky.

---------- ❖ ❖ ❖ ----------

Woe Unto You, O Dinâr

There is an interesting story related about Dinâr Al-
'Ayyâr. Dinâr had a righteous mother who would
constantly advise him to repent for his wayward, sinful
existence, but as much as she tried, her words had no
positive effect on him whatsoever. Then, one day, as he
was walking by a graveyard, he stopped to pick up a
bone; he was shocked to see how it crumbled and turned
to dust in his hand. The sight of that bone had a profound
effect on Dinâr. He began to think about his life and his
past sins, and he then exclaimed, "Woe unto you, O
Dinâr, you are going to end up like this crushed bone, and
your body will turn into dust." All of his past sins then
flashed before his eyes, and he made a firm resolve to
repent. Turning his gaze towards the sky, he said, "My
Lord, I now turn to You in complete submission, so accept
me and have mercy on me."

With a completely changed heart and state of mind, Dinâr
went to his mother and said, "Mother, what does a master
do when he captures his slave, who had run away from
him?" She said, "(To punish him,) the master then
provides him with coarse clothing and low-quality food;
and he ties his hands and feet, so that he does not make
another attempt to escape." Dinâr said, "Then I want a
garment made of coarse wool, low-quality barley, and
two chains. Mother, do with me that which is done to a

runaway slave: Perhaps my Lord will, upon seeing my
humiliation and humility, have mercy on me." Seeing
that her son was adamant and resolute in his request, she
complied.

At the beginning of every ensuing night, Dinâr would
begin to cry and wail uncontrollably. And he would
continue to repeat to himself the words: "Woe unto you,
O Dinâr, do you have the power to withstand the Hell-
fire! How brazen you have been to have led a life that has
made you deserving of the anger of the All-Mighty!" He
would continue upon that state until the morning.
Turning wan and pale, Dinâr's body slowly wasted
away. Not being able to bear seeing him in that pitiable
state, his mother said, "My son, be easy on yourself." He
answered, "My mother, let me remain tired for a short
while, so that perhaps I can achieve long-term comfort
later on. For tomorrow, I will be waiting a long time
before my Majestic Lord, and I do not know whether He
will order me to go to places of beautiful shade or to
places of unspeakable horror."

She said, "My son, at least rest for a while." He said, "It is
not present rest or comfort that I am seeking out. Mother,
it is as if I see you and other people being led tomorrow
towards Paradise, while I am being led towards the Hell-
fire along with its inhabitants." She left him then, and he
returned to crying, worshiping, and reciting the Qur'ân.
One night, as he was reciting the Qur'ân, he came across
these Verses:

$$﴿ فَوَرَبِّكَ لَنَسْـَٔلَنَّهُمْ أَجْمَعِينَ ۝ عَمَّا كَانُوا۟ يَعْمَلُونَ ۝﴾$$

"So, by your Lord (O Muhammad (ﷺ)), We shall

certainly call all of them to account, For all that they used to do.''[1]

As he contemplated the meanings and implications of the Verses, he cried with such intensity that he fainted. His mother rushed to him and tried very hard to revive him, but he wouldn't respond; she thought that he had died. Looking into the face of her precious son, she said, "O my beloved one, O the joy of my heart, where shall we meet again?" In fact, Dinâr still had some life left in him, and hearing his mother's words, he answered with a faint voice, "My mother, if you do not find me on the wide plains of the Resurrection Day, then ask Malik, the Custodian of the Hell-fire, about me." He then made a croaking sound and died.

After she finished washing his body, Dinâr's mother prepared him for his funeral. She then went out and made the announcement: "O people, come to the (funeral) prayer of one who has been killed by (fear of) the Hell-fire." People began to come from all directions; it is said that, during that era, no greater gathering came together and no amount of tears were shed as much as on that day.

On the same night that his funeral was held, one of Dinâr's friends saw him in a dream: attired in a green robe, Dinâr was prancing around in Paradise, all the while reciting theVerse:

$$﴿ فَوَرَبِّكَ لَنَسْـَٔلَنَّهُمْ أَجْمَعِينَ ۝ عَمَّا كَانُوا۟ يَعْمَلُونَ ۝ ﴾$$

"So, by your Lord [O Muhammad (ﷺ)], We shall certainly call all of them to account, for all that they used

---

[1] *Qur'ân* 15:92, 93

to do.''[1]

During the dream, his friend heard him say, "By His Might and Majesty, He asked me (about my deeds). Having mercy on me, He forgave me and pardoned me (my sins). Lo! Convey news of this to my mother."

---------- ❖ ❖ ❖ ----------

---

[1] *Qur'ân* 15:92, 93

Coming To Terms With
The Reality Of Life

It is reported that there was once a king who, at a certain moment during his rule, came to the realization that no matter how rich he was, his pleasures were of the fleeting kind and his end was going to be death. These thoughts lingered in his mind, until one day he secretly left his castle and made his way towards the seaside. There he spent his days earning his keep by working with bricks, and his nights worshiping Allâh (﷾). Although he had traveled far away from his homeland, he could not remain unrecognized for long, and soon news of his story reached the king of the land that he was in. That king summoned him, but he refused to go; and when he was summoned for a second time, he made it clear that he didn't want to meet the king.

The king of that land was too curious about the former king's story to let the matter rest there. And so he went to him in person, but when the former king saw him approaching, he began to run away. The king of the land chased him as he called out, "O slave of Allâh, fear not (for I have no intention of harming you)," but the former king continued to flee from him. This continued until the king of the land was able to convince him that he just wanted to talk to him for a few moments. When the two were face to face, the king of the land asked the former king, "What made you want to come to this land (and live the life you are leading)?"

He said, "I found that my heart desired separation from the children of Adam." The king of the land asked, "How can you bear living a life of loneliness?" He said, "Whoever finds comfort with Allâh finds unwholesome the company of anyone else." The king of the land asked, "And why did you leave your realm?"

He answered, "I thought about my outcome, my final destination on this earth, and I realized that my end here was near at hand. And so I decided to turn away from that which is temporary and to instead turn towards that which will abide forever. Turning to my Lord, I then fled from my sins." The king of the land said, "You do not have more reason than I do to fear Allâh (ﷻ)." The king of that land then abdicated his throne, after which he followed his new companion on the path of simplicity, repentance, and worship.

---------- ❖ ❖ ❖ ----------

You Have Guided Me To A Path That You Know Not Yourselves

The following story is narrated by 'Abdul-Wâhid bin Zaid:

We were on a sea vessel once, when the wind suddenly became tempestuous, and we were forced to leave the high seas and seek refuge on an island. We were surprised to see that we were not alone on the island; there standing before us was a man who was busy worshiping an idol. We introduced ourselves and then said, "We do not have anyone on our ship that does as you are doing." The man asked, "Then who is it that you worship?" We said, "We worship Allâh (ﷻ)." He asked, "And who is Allâh?" We said, "He Whose Throne is in the heavens, and Whose dominion is the heavens, the earth, and all that exists."

"And how did you come to know that?" asked the man.

"He sent a Messenger to us with clear proofs and miracles, and it was that Messenger who informed us about Him."

"And what has happened to your Messenger?"

"When he finished conveying the message, Allâh caused him to die," we answered.

"Has he left you no sign?" asked the man.

"He (ﷺ) has left among us Allâh's Book," we said.

"Show it to me," requested the man. When we showed him a copy of the Qur'ân, he said, "I cannot read it," and so we read a part of it for him. He then cried and said, "The One Whose speech this is must not be disobeyed." Not only did the man then accept Islam; he also assiduously learned its teachings and then put what he learned into practice. When the weather calmed down and we were ready to leave the island, he asked us if he could be a passenger on our ship. We of course agreed to have him join us, and it was a good thing that he came with us, for it gave us the opportunity to teach him a number of Chapters of the Qur'ân. At the end of the first evening of travel, all of us crewmen got ready to go to sleep. Our new passenger said, "O people, the Lord that you guided me to, does He sleep?" We said, "He is the Ever Living, the One Who sustains and protects all that exists. Neither slumber, nor sleep overtake Him." He looked at us and said, "It is indeed bad manners for a slave to sleep in the presence of his master." With a great deal of energy and vigor, he then jumped up and began to pray; and his crying voice could be heard until the morning.

When we reached a place called 'Abâdân, I said to my companions, "The man is a stranger here; moreover, he is a new Muslim. We would do well to gather some money for him in order to help him out." We gathered what we could, but when we tried to give him the money, he exclaimed, "What is this!" We said, "Money that you can spend on yourself." He said, "How perfect Allâh is! You have guided me to a way that you do not know yourselves. When I was living on a barren desert in the middle of the ocean, I worshiped other than Him, yet He did not allow me to go without; then how is it possible that He will make me be needy, when it is Him alone that I now worship. Indeed He is the Creator and the All-Provider." He then left us and went on his way.

A number of days passed before we heard any news of his whereabouts. We were told that he was in such and such place and that he was extremely sick. When we reached him, we saw that he was on the verge of dying. After extending greetings of peace to him, I said, "Do you need anything?" He said, "The One Who brought you to the island when I did not know Him has provided me with all that I need."

---------- ❖ ❖ ❖ ----------

What I Want Is Life That Is Not Ended By Death

It is reported that during one of his journeys, Dhul-Qarnain passed through a city that was once ruled by seven successive kings. Upon meeting some of the inhabitants of the city, Dhul-Qarnain asked, "Are any of the descendents of those kings alive today?" They said, "Yes, a single male descendent, yet he steers clear of human beings and keeps company with no one; in fact, he spends much of his time in the graveyard." Dhul-Qarnain said, "Tell me where I can find him." He then went to meet with the eccentric-sounding of kings. When he finally met him, he noticed that he looked weak and had an emaciated body. Though Dhul-Qarnain didn't know it, the man's body was so thin not from a lack of resources, but from constant worship and a general lack of concern for material pleasures. Dhul-Qarnain extended greetings of peace to the man, who then returned those greetings. Dhul-Qarnain then asked, "Why do you spend so much time in the graveyard?" The man lowered his head for a moment, and after a brief pause, he raised it and said, "I initially wanted to see if I could distinguish between the bones of kings and the bones of their slaves, but of course I wasn't able to do so. Their end is the same."

Dhul-Qarnain said, "If you wish to follow me, I will help you to rekindle the honor of your fathers — that is, if you have the ambition that is needed to achieve that end." The man said, "My ambition for that is little. But if you really want to help me." Dhul-Qarnain said, "What is it that you desire (and I will then try to help you to achieve your goal)?" He said, "What I want is life that is not ended by death, youth that is never supplanted by old age, and richness that is never followed by poverty."

"I cannot help you achieve that end," said Dhul-Qarnain. The man said, "Then go on to your business, and leave me to seek the fulfillment of my goal from He Who is able to help me. For indeed, this world is departing, and the Hereafter draws near. The journey is long, yet I have not much provision (i.e., good deeds) for it."

---------- ❖ ❖ ❖ ----------

The True Treasure

A burglar scaled the fence of Mâlik bin Dinâr's home and easily managed to get inside. Once inside the house, the burglar was disappointed to see that there was nothing inside actually worth stealing. The owner of the home was inside at the time; he was busy performing prayer. Realizing that he was not alone, Mâlik quickly ended his prayer and turned around to face the burglar. Without showing any sign of being shocked or afraid, Mâlik calmly extended greetings of peace and then said, "My brother, may Allâh forgive you. You entered my home and found nothing that is worth taking, yet I do not want you to leave my home without taking away some benefit." He stood up, went to another part of the room, and came back with a jug full of water. He looked intently into the eyes of the burglar and said, "Make ablution and perform two units of prayer, for if you do so, you will leave my home with a greater treasure than you had initially sought when you entered it." Much humbled by Mâlik's manners and words, the burglar said, "Yes, that is a generous offer indeed." After making ablution and performing two units of prayer, the burglar said, "O Mâlik, would you mind if I stayed a while, for I want to stay to perform two more units of prayer?" Mâlik said, " Stay for whatever amount of prayer Allâh decrees for you to perform now." The burglar ended up spending the entire night at Mâlik's house; he continued to pray until the morning. Then Mâlik said, "Leave now and be good." But instead of leaving, the burglar said, "Would you mind if I stayed here with you today, for I have made an intention to fast the day?"

"Stay as long as you wish," said Mâlik. The burglar ended up staying for a number of days, praying during the late hours of each night and fasting throughout the duration of each day. When he finally decided to leave, the burglar said, "O Mâlik, I have made a firm resolve to repent for my sins and for my former way of life." Mâlik said, "Indeed that is in the Hand of Allâh." True to his word and promise, the burglar repented and began to lead a life of righteousness and obedience to Allâh (ﷻ). Later on, he met up with one of his former burglar friends, who said to him, "Have you found your treasure yet?" He said, "My brother, what I found is Mâlik bin Dinâr: I went to steal from him, but it was he who ended up stealing (my heart). I have indeed repented to Allâh, and I will continue to strive until I achieve what the righteous ones have achieved."

---------- ❖ ❖ ❖ ----------

The Accepted Repentance

A man once went to Râbi'ah bint Ismâ'il Al-'Adawiyyah, who was known by the titles, ' Mother of Goodness,' and, 'The Famous Worshiper.' He said, "Indeed, I have perpetrated a great number of sins. If I repent, do you think that Allâh will accept my repentance?" She said, "Woe unto you! Do you not see that He invites those who turn away from Him; then why wouldn't He accept the repentance of those who turn towards Him?"

What she said is indeed true, for Allâh (ﷻ) is happy when we submit to Him and hasten back to Him, repentant for our sins. To worship Him is the purpose for which we were created. Glad tidings, then, to he who knows his purpose and puts what he knows into practice.

---------- ❖ ❖ ❖ ----------

Good Advice

During one of his journeys, Sari As-Saqati passed by a cave, from which he heard the sound of continuous sobbing. Aroused by curiosity, he entered the cave and saw a young man whose body seemed to be wasted away by grief and sadness. Having immediately perceived that the man was a righteous worshipper, Sari humbly asked, "O young man, how is safety achieved?" He said, "By performing all prescribed acts of worship, by not wronging others, and by repenting to Allâh (ﷻ)." Sari asked, "Can you please deliver a sermon to me?"

The young man said, "The best sermon you can receive is by looking into your own self. But I will say this: be obedient to Allâh when you are alone, for doing so will atone for your sins, and Allâh (ﷻ) will then display you to the inhabitants of the heavens."

---------- ❖ ❖ ❖ ----------

Good Deeds Actually
Remove Evil Deeds

A righteous man was once asked to tell the story of the pivotal moment of his life, the moment in which he first began to apply the teachings of Islam, and the following was his answer:

When I was a young man, I would not hesitate to perpetrate any sin that was made available to me. Then, one day, I saw a young woman who was perhaps the most beautiful woman that I had ever seen. Much tempted by her, I indicated to her that I wanted her to approach me. She seemed nervous, but I thought that she would probably agree to satisfy my sexual desires for money. She approached me with what seemed to be a great deal of trepidation, and when she actually stood before me, she looked extremely terrified. Feeling sorry for her, I said, "Do not fear, for I will not harm you." But my words did not lessen her terrible fright in the least; in fact, her situation worsened: she began to tremble like a palm tree leaf trembles with the wind. I said, "Tell me your story." She said, "By Allâh, O my brother, never before this day have I offered my body in this way. Dire need is what has driven me to this, for I have three daughters who have not eaten a single morsel of food for three days now. It was pity for them that brought me to this low point in my life." Something then happened to me that had never happened to me before: I felt sorry for another human being. After she told me where she lived, I took a great deal of money, clothing, and food to her house. When I returned to my house, I told my mother what had happened. My mother knew that I had a book in which I would record all of my evil exploits, and so she said to me, "My son, you are a man who has never performed a good deed except for the good deed that you performed today. I know that you have a book in which you record your evil exploits; go now and write in it your good deed." I stood up, went to my book, opened it, and found that all of its pages were blank – except for the first page on which was written a single line. These were the words that I saw before me on that line:

$$﴿ إِنَّ ٱلْحَسَنَٰتِ يُذْهِبْنَ ٱلسَّيِّئَاتِ ﴾$$

"Verily, the good deeds remove the evil deeds (i.e. small sins)."[1]

At that very moment, I raised my hands to the sky and said, "By Your Might and Majesty, never again will I disobey You."

---

[1] *Qur'ân* 11:114

The Grave Of A Righteous Man

Ibrâhim bin Bashshâr narrated this story:

While I was walking towards Kufah with Ibrâhim bin Adham, he stopped beside a grave and invoked Allâh (ﷻ) to have mercy on its dweller. "Whose grave is this?" I asked.

"It is the grave of Humaid bin Jâbir," said Ibrâhim. "He was once the leader of all of the townships that are in this area."

"What was so special about him (that made you stop here in order to supplicate for him)?" I asked. Ibrâhim told me that he was a very rich leader, who would spend his nights enjoying frivolous games and entertainment.

"One night he fell asleep and saw a dream in which a man was standing over his head," said Ibrâhim. "The man had a book in his hand, which Humaid grabbed and tore open. The words inside were written with gold (ink); they ran as follows: Do not prefer My Fire over My Light, and do not be deceived by what you own in this world, for what you own is preventing you from getting what I saved for you in your afterlife. True, what you have might have been called a kingdom, had it not been for the fact that all of it will soon perish. And your life might have been called a life of happiness and joy, had it not been for the fact that it will be followed by anxiety and misery. So beware of falling under the spell of these worldly ornaments, or you will join the ranks of the destroyed ones.

$$\text{﴿وَسَارِعُوٓا۟ إِلَىٰ مَغْفِرَةٍ مِّن رَّبِّكُمْ وَجَنَّةٍ عَرْضُهَا ٱلسَّمَـٰوَٰتُ وَٱلْأَرْضُ أُعِدَّتْ لِلْمُتَّقِينَ ١٣٣﴾}$$

"And march forth in the way (which leads to) forgiveness from your Lord, and for Paradise as wide as are the heavens and the earth, prepared for Al-Muttaqûn (the righteous)."[1]

"Humaid then woke up in a terrified state," continued Ibrâhim. "Resigning from his post as leader, Humaid betook himself to this mountain, where he led a simple life, doing menial work to maintain his physical upkeep, but dedicating most of his time to the worship of Allâh (ﷻ). I came here once and met him; by keeping company with him, I found him to be a noble man. I would thereafter continue to visit him until he died."

---

[1] *Qur'ân* 3:133.

Mercy And Forgiveness For The One Who Repents

When Al-Mansûr bin 'Ammâr (may Allâh have mercy on him) once entered the court of 'Abdul-Malik bin Marwân, the latter said, "O Mansûr, I have a question for you, and I will give you respite for an entire year to answer it: Who is the wisest of people, and who is the most ignorant of people?"

Al-Mansûr left the castle and spent some time in contemplation in a nearby courtyard. Then the answer came to him, and so he quickly hurried back to 'Abdul-Malik. "O Mansûr, why have you returned?" asked 'Abdul-Malik.

"The wisest of people, O Leader of the Believers, is the doer of good deeds who fears (not having his deeds accepted)," said Al-Mansûr. "And the most ignorant of people is he who does good deeds and feels safe (in that his deeds will be accepted)." Upon hearing these words, 'Abdul-Malik began to cry until his garment became soaked in tears. He then said, "You have done well, O Mansûr. Now recite a part of the Qur'ân to me, for the Qur'ân is a cure for what is in the breasts of men." Mansûr then recited this Verse:

﴿يَوْمَ تَجِدُ كُلُّ نَفْسٍ مَّا عَمِلَتْ مِنْ خَيْرٍ مُّحْضَرًا وَمَا عَمِلَتْ مِن سُوءٍ تَوَدُّ

لَوْ أَنَّ بَيْنَهَا وَبَيْنَهُۥ أَمَدَۢا بَعِيدًا ۗ وَيُحَذِّرُكُمُ ٱللَّهُ نَفْسَهُ ۗ وَٱللَّهُ رَءُوفُۢ بِٱلْعِبَادِ

﴿٣٠﴾

"On the Day when every person will be confronted with all the good he has done, and all the evil he has done, he will wish that there were a great distance between him and his evil. And Allâh warns you against Himself and Allâh is full of Kindness to (His) slaves."[1]

"You have killed me, O Mansûr," said 'Abdul-Malik. "O Mansûr, what does, 'And Allâh warns you against Himself,' mean?"

"It means His Punishment," said Mansûr.

"And what is the meaning of 'every person will be confronted with all the good he has done'?" asked 'Abdul-Malik.

"It means that every person will be confronted on the Day of Resurrection by all of his deeds, the largest of them and the tiniest of them. Allâh (ﷻ) will not leave out or forget any of that." 'Abdul-Malik then continued to cry until, being overcome with fear, he fainted.

---------- ❖ ❖ ❖ ----------

---

[1] *Qur'ân* 3:30

Everything That Is Going To Happen Is Near At Hand

This is one of the famous sayings of Al-Hasan (may Allâh have mercy on him): "Before He created us, Allâh (﷾) knew that we would sin and disobey him; yet He (﷾) still made us Muslims. O sinners, hurry to repent before the pangs of death overcome you, before the time of utter regret is upon you. Work, for death is coming, and everything that is coming is near at hand. Death hovers over you day and night; it will not come late, not even for one who has lost track of time (i.e., although the one who loses track of time is late for all of his appointments, he will not be late for his appointment with death)."

---------- ❖ ❖ ❖ ----------

Let Us Hasten To Repent

Death may come upon us at any time, and it is our last deed that counts most: Put together, these two realities make it clear that we must continually repent for our sins and that it is utter foolishness to put off repentance for another day.

In relation to this point, there is an interesting story related about two brothers. One of them, who lived on the top floor of a house they shared together, was a pious worshipper; the other, who lived on the ground floor, was a prolific doer of evil deeds. The former was confident – in fact, a little too confident and self-complacent for his own good. He actually desired that the Devil should try to tempt him, so that he could resist temptation and soar to higher levels of righteousness. One day, the Devil did appear before him, perhaps in the form of a man (it is not mentioned in the narration). The Devil said, "So very sad that you have spent 40 years inhibiting the satisfaction of your desires and tiring your body in worship. You have 40 more years left to live, you know; why don't you enjoy yourself and follow your lusts for a while. Then you can always repent and return to worship later on. After all, Allâh is Most-Forgiving, Most Merciful."

The worshipper thought to himself: "I will go down to my brother on the first floor, and I will join him in the pursuit of pleasure for 20 years. Then, in the last 20 years of my life, I will repent to Allâh (ﷻ) and worship Him." He then began to descend the stairs to the first floor.

Meanwhile, his brother was going through a transformation of his own. He thought to himself: "I wasted away my entire life in sin. My brother, the worshipper, will enter Paradise, while I will enter the Hell-fire. By Allâh, I will indeed repent, go up to my brother, and join him, for as long as I live, in the worship of Allâh (ﷻ). Perhaps Allâh will then forgive me."

He ascended the stairs, with the intention of repenting to Allâh (ﷻ), while his brother was descending with the intention of leading a life of sin. The latter slipped on one of the stairs, tumbled down, and knocked down his brother. Both of them died.

I mentioned it earlier, and I'll mention it here again: It is, of course, the last deed that counts most.

---------- ❖ ❖ ❖ ----------

If You Really Want
To Disobey Allâh...!

It is reported that a man once went to Ibrâhim bin Adham and said, "O Abu Ishâq, I continually wrong my own self, and I turn away from everything that invites me to improve my way of life."

Ibrâhim said, "If you can fulfill five conditions, then sinning will never harm you, and you can fulfill your desires as much as you want."

"Tell me those conditions," exclaimed the man.

"As for the first, if you want to disobey Allâh (ﷻ), then do not eat from His sustenance," said Ibrâhim.

"What then will I eat, for everything on the earth is from His sustenance?" said the man.

"Listen," said Ibrâhim. "Are you being sensible when you eat from His sustenance while you are disobedient to Him?"

"No," said the man. "What is the second condition?" he asked, somewhat nervously.

"If you want to disobey Allâh, then do not live in any of His lands," said Ibrâhim.

"This is even worse than the first. All that is in the East and West belong to Him. So where then will I live?"

"Listen," said Ibrâhim. "If you insist on disobeying Him while you eat from His sustenance and live in His lands, then at least look for some spot where He cannot see you, and disobey Him there."

"O Ibrâhim!" exclaimed the man. "How can I do that, when He (ﷻ) even knows the deepest secrets that are in the breasts of men? What is the fourth condition?" he asked, downright despondently.

"When the angel of death comes to take your soul, then say to him, 'Give me some respite, so that I can repent sincerely and perform good deeds.'"

"When the time comes, the angel will not accept that plea from me," said the man.

"Listen," said Ibrâhim. "If you cannot put off death in order to repent, then how do you expect to be saved?"

"Tell me the fifth condition," said the man.

"When the guardians of the Hell-fire come to take you away on the Day of Resurrection, don't go with them."

"They won't let me go!" exclaimed the man.

"Then how do you expect to be saved?" asked Ibrâhim.

"Stop, stop! That is enough for me," said the man. "I ask Allâh to forgive me, and I indeed repent to Him." From that day onwards, he dedicated his life to the worship of Allâh (ﷻ).

---------- ❖ ❖ ❖ ----------

The Lingering Pain Of Sinning

To be sure, every single one of us is a sinner. But what distinguishes some from others is that some people feel no remorse for past sins, while others feel a great deal of remorse. The latter group repents and continually strives to improve, while the former group sits back self-complacently, going through the motions of life without appreciating the significance of their actions.

For a sincere person, sin is painful; its pain lingers in his heart for many years, very often until the day he dies. An example of such a person is the noble Companion, Sa'id bin 'Âmir (رضى الله عنه).

During the caliphate of 'Umar bin Al-Khattâb (رضى الله عنه), Sa'id bin 'Âmir (رضى الله عنه) was the governor of Hims, a city in Ash-Shâm. When 'Umar (رضى الله عنه) visited Hims to see how things were going there, he was met by a large group of people who began to complain to him about Sa'id (رضى الله عنه). Basically, they found fault with Sa'id (رضى الله عنه) in four matters. First, they said, he would not come out to them until mid-morning. Second, he would refuse to answer any caller during the night. Third, once a month, he would stay away from the people. And fourth, every once in a while, Sa'id (رضى الله عنه) would faint and lose consciousness for no apparent reason.

The Leader of the Believers asked Sa'id (رضى الله عنه) to respond to their complaints. In regard to the first complaint, Sa'id (رضى الله عنه)

explained that he had no servant and that, every morning, he had to crush his own wheat in order to make bread. As soon as he would finish making his bread, he said, he would then go out to serve the people. As for not answering any callers during the night, he said that he dedicated his days to serving the people, and his nights to worshiping Allâh (). As for not going out to the people once a month, he explained that he had only one garment and that he washed it once a month and had to then wait until it dried.

As for passing out every so often, Sa'id () gave this explanation: "When I was a polytheist, I witnessed the brutal execution of Habib Al-Ansâri in Makkah. I saw how the Quraish cut up his flesh (little by little). They said (to Habib), 'Do you now want for Muhammad to take your place?' He said, 'By Allâh, I would not want to be safe with my self, my family, and my children, if Muhammad were even to be pricked by a thorn.' Every time I remember that day and how I refrained from helping Habib – for I was a polytheist and did not believe in Allâh, the All-Mighty – I begin to think that Allâh *'Azza wa-Jall* (the Possessor of might and majesty) will never forgive me. It is then that I (faint), O Leader of the Believers."

---------- ❖ ❖ ❖ ----------

The Integrity of
Fudail bin 'Iyâd (رضي الله عنه)

Ar-Rashid, a first century ruler, once said to Fudail bin 'Iyâd, "Admonish me."

"O Leader of the Believers!" said Fudail. "Indeed, your grandfather, Al-'Abbâs (رضي الله عنه), the uncle of the Prophet (ﷺ), once went to the Prophet (ﷺ) and said, 'O Messenger of Allâh, appoint me to be a leader.' The Messenger of Allâh (ﷺ) said:

«يَا عَمِّ. . . نَفْسٌ تُحْيِيهَا خَيْرٌ مِنْ إِمَارَةٍ لا تُحْصِيهَا. . . إِنَّ الإِمَارَةَ حَسْرَةٌ. . . وَنَدَامَةٌ. . . يَوْمَ الْقِيَامَةِ. . . فَإِنِ اسْتَطَعْتِ أَلَّا تَكُونَ أَمِيرًا فَافْعَلْ!»

'My uncle... indeed, being a leader leads to... sorrow... and regret... on the Day of Resurrection... If you are able to go (to live your life) without (ever) being a leader, then do so!'

Moved to tears, Ar-Rashid said, "Give me more."

Fudail looked intently at Ar-Rashid and said, "O one who has a handsome face, if you are able to protect that face from the Hell-fire, then do so. And beware of ever cheating or betraying your people." Being much moved by Fudail's words, Ar-Rashid wanted to reward him. "Do you have any debts?" he asked.

"To my Lord, yes, and He will hold me accountable for

them," said Fudail.

"I am of course referring to debts to other human beings," said Ar-Rashid. After Fudail answered in the negative, Ar-Rashid said to one of his assistants, "Give him 1000 dinars, which he can use to help his family." Al-Fudail was greatly offended by these words: "How perfect Allâh is!" he exclaimed. "I am guiding you to (ultimate) safety, and you want to reward me with this (paltry, worldly sum)!" He then left, having refused to take anything.

---------- ❖ ❖ ❖ ----------

Death Is Better Than
Allâh's Punishment

(The following story is simple enough, yet it teaches us two important lessons. First, when you make an intention to sin, you can still save yourself by backing down, even if you do so at the very last moment. Second, you can avoid certain sins but still fulfill your desires if you take an alternative lawful path. – Editor)

A very rich businessman was once relaxing in his home when he heard someone knock on his door. When he opened the door, there standing before him was the most beautiful girl that he had ever seen in his entire life. He yearned for her and invited her to come inside. But it was not to fulfill his desires that she came; rather, she came because she was extremely poor and was forced to go around begging for money. He ignored her plea for help and instead insisted that she come inside. She answered him in a clear and dignified tone: "Death is better than disobeying my Lord." She left but then returned after a number of days. Her situation had obviously become more desperate, and again she asked him to help her. The businessman answered her as he did the first time.

With tears flowing down her cheeks, the girl entered his house; he was now ever so close to utter ruin. Again she pleaded: "Please! Feed me for the Countenance of Allâh!"

"Not unless you allow me to satisfy my desires with

you," said the man, both coldly and hungrily.

"Death is better than the punishment of Allâh," proclaimed the girl. As she was leaving, her sincere words echoed in the mind of the businessman, and after a long life of sinning, sincere tears of remorse flowed from his eyes for the very first time. He repented to Allâh (﷾) and then fed the girl. He then married her, and they enjoyed a happy marriage together. (You see, in the end, he got what he wanted, except that he got it in a lawful manner. And that is what made all the difference.)

---------- ❖ ❖ ❖ ----------

The Evil, Long-Term Effects Of Sinning ... Yet There Is Hope Until The Very End

One day, as 'Ali bin Abu Tâlib (⬥) and Al-Husain bin 'Ali (⬥) were walking together, they heard a man supplicating to Allâh (⬥). The man was begging Allâh (⬥) to forgive him for his evil crimes. His sincere tone and eloquent words aroused the interest of 'Ali (⬥), who turned to his son and said, "Do you not hear the man who is so very contrite because of his sins. Go catch up with him and call him (hither)." When Al-Husain (⬥) caught up with the man, he saw that he was clean-looking, clean-smelling, with nice clothes and altogether handsome – except that he seemed to be paralyzed on the right side of his body. Al-Husain (⬥) said, "Answer the summons of the Leader of the Believers, 'Ali bin Abu Tâlib (⬥)."

Dragging his right side, the man followed Al-Husain (⬥) back to where 'Ali (⬥) was waiting for them. "Who are you? And what is your story?" asked 'Ali (⬥).

"My story is that of a man who did not fulfill the rights of others and is now being punished for that," said the man.

"And what is your name?" asked 'Ali (⬥).

"Munâzil bin Lâhiq," said the man.

"And what is your story?" asked 'Ali (⬥).

The man then told him his story, which is, in abridged

form, as follows: "I was famous among the Arabs for my frivolous and sinful exploits. Merciful and kind, my father would constantly admonish me and advise me to mend my ways. He would remind me of Allâh's punishment, saying, 'My son' do not go against He Who punishes with the Hell-fire!' When he would persist in advising me, I felt his voice grating on my nerves. I would get so frustrated that I would beat him with harsh blows. In response to my blows, he one day said, 'By Allâh, I will fast, without breaking my fast; and I will pray without stopping to sleep.' He fasted for entire week, but seeing no change in my behavior, he climbed a camel and set off to perform *Hajj*. His parting words were, "I am going to the House of Allâh, and there I will seek help from Allâh against you." When he reached Makkah, he embraced the curtain of the Ka'bah and supplicated against me, asking Allâh (ﷻ) to make me paralyzed on one side of my body. By the One Who raised the sky and sends down rain, no sooner did my father finish his supplication than I became paralyzed on my right side, which became like a piece of wood. Anyone that would then pass by me would point to me and say, 'Allâh answered his father's supplication against him.'"

"What did your father do then?" 'Ali (ﷺ) asked.

"O Leader of the Believers, after he became pleased with me, I asked him to go back (to the Ka'bah) and invoke Allâh on my behalf. He agreed to do so. I walked alongside him as he rode on his camel, until we reached a place called, the Valley of Arak. When we reached there, a group of birds flew away from a tree; their sudden movement frightened the camel. As the camel raced off in a state of fright, my father fell off of it and died."

It was certainly late for the man, but not too late, and so 'Ali (🙏) advised him to continue to supplicate and to repent for his past misdeeds. 'Ali (🙏) then parted from the man, but before leaving him, he taught him the supplication that a person who is in distress should say. The narration does not specifically mention which supplication it was that 'Ali (🙏) taught the man; nonetheless, here are some Prophetic supplications that those in distress can say:

● "None has the right to be worshiped except Allâh, the All-Mighty, the Most Forbearing. None has the right to be worshiped except Allâh, Lord of the magnificent throne. None has the right to be worshiped except Allâh, Lord of the heavens, Lord of the earth and Lord of the noble throne."

● "O Allâh, it is Your mercy that I hope for, so do not leave me in charge of my affairs even for a blink of an eye and rectify for me all of my affairs. None has the right to be worshiped except You.'

● "None has the right to be worshiped except You. How perfect You are, verily I was among the wrong-doers."

● "O Allâh, there is no ease except in that which You have made easy, and You make the difficulty, if You wish, easy."

---------- ❖ ❖ ❖ ----------

The Noble Qur'ân

One year, when Al-Asma'i was on his way to perform *Hajj*, a Bedouin who carried a large sword and a long spear confronted him. It was quite obvious that he was a highway robber. He came near Al-Asma'i, and instead of fleeing or attempting to escape, Al-Asma'i drew nearer to him. Without any show of nervousness or trepidation, Al-Asma'i extended greetings of peace to the robber. The latter responded and then asked, "Where are you from?"

"I am a poor man on a journey," was Al-Asma'i reply, though it did not really answer the robber's question.

"Do you have anything with you?" asked the robber politely. He probably thought: If he is going to address me with good manners, I might as well rob him with a show of proper etiquette.

"Yes, I have with me the Qur'ân," answered Al-Asma'i.

"And what is the Qur'ân?" asked the robber, who obviously had never before heard of Islam.

"It is the speech of Allâh *'Azza wa-Jall* (the Possessor of might and majesty)," said Al-Asma'i.

"And does Allâh have speech?"

"Yes," replied Al-Asma'i.

"Then let me hear some of His speech," said the robber. Al-Asma'i then recited the following Verse:

﴿وَفِي ٱلسَّمَاءِ رِزْقُكُمْ وَمَا تُوعَدُونَ ٢٢﴾

"And in the heaven is your provision, and that which you are promised."[1]

When the robber heard these words, he began to cry, after which he threw down his sword and spear. He then said, "Perish the highway robber, who seeks sustenance on earth, when it is really in the heavens!" Realizing that his sustenance was guaranteed by Allâh (ﷻ), the robber immediately perceived the utter folly of seeking out sustenance through unlawful means. And so he repented and made a vow never to return to that sin again.

Al-Asma'i was very much pleased to see the quick and complete transformation of the robber. On the following year, when Al-Asma'i went to perform *Hajj* again, he saw the former robber – whose face now had the signs of Faith written on it – clinging to the curtain of the Ka'bah. It was late in the night and he was saying, "O my Lord eyes are sleeping and every loved one is with his beloved. The gates of all kings are now closed, but Your gate is open to those who ask of You. Would that I knew whether You accepted this night (of worship) from me..."

---------- ❖ ❖ ❖ ----------

---

[1] *Qur'ân* 51:22

A Tongue That Remains Moist With The Remembrance Of Allâh (ﷻ)

When passing through a mountain-pass, a Bedouin once came across an old man who was blind and who seemed to be afflicted with various ailments all over his body; it was clear that he was wasting away. He was even paralyzed and was consequently forced to remain in a seated position. The Bedouin could distinctly hear him say: "All praise is for Allâh, Who has kept me safe from ailments with which He has tested many among His creation; and He has indeed preferred me over many among those that He (ﷻ) created."

"My brother!" exclaimed the Bedouin. "What have you been saved from? By Allâh, I think that you have been afflicted with every single kind of ailment!"

"Go away from me," said the old man, as he raised his head. "Do I not still have a tongue with which I can pronounce His Oneness, and with which I can remember Him every single moment? And do I not still have a heart with which I can know Him?" These words of the old man had a profound effect on the Bedouin. He immediately repented to Allâh (ﷻ) for his sins and asked Allâh (ﷻ) for forgiveness.

---------- ❖ ❖ ❖ ----------

Race Towards Repentance!

Wanting to advise his son Al-Hasan (﷦), 'Ali (﷦) said, "My son: Beware of three; be in harmony with three; be modest before three; race to three; flee from three; be in disagreement with three; fear three; and hope from three."

"O my father, please explain," said Al-Hasan (﷦).

"Beware of pride, anger, and the base kind of ambition. Live in harmony with Allâh's Book, His Messenger's *Sunnah,* and the lives of His righteous slaves. Be modest before Allâh, the angels, and righteous people. Hurry away [to someplace (away from sinning)] from fear of sinning, race to repentance, and sprint forward in the pursuit of knowledge. My son, flee from lying, treachery, and transgression. Stay away from (i.e., be in disagreement with) evil and its people, hypocrisy and its people, and foolishness and its people. Fear Allâh, (the company of) those who do not fear Allâh, and the biting (evil speech) of your tongue. Hope for Allâh to forgive your sins, to accept your deeds, and to accept the intercession of your Prophet (ﷺ)."

---------- ❖ ❖ ❖ ----------

The Ever-Living Never Sleeps

Both of them lived in a small town that was populated by only tens or hundreds of people. He was in love with her, and so when he saw her walking alone one night, he followed her until he had her cornered. When he came near to her, he said, 'Woman, I crave for you.' She said, 'First go and see if all of the people are asleep.' Very much pleased at her response, for it seemed as if she reciprocated his desire, he walked around the town and then returned. "Everyone is asleep," he said.

"What about Allâh *'Azza wa-Jall* (the Possessor of might and majesty)?" she asked. "Is He sleeping at this hour?"

"Woman, what are you saying?" he exclaimed. "Indeed, Allâh does not sleep: Neither slumber, nor sleep overtake Him."

"The One Who hasn't slept and doesn't sleep sees us, even if people don't see us," she said. "Do you not fear He Who neither sleeps nor is heedless (of anything that happens)?"

Simple though he was, the man grasped her point; moreover, he was deeply moved by her words. With tears flowing from his eyes, he left her alone, having nothing in his mind except the desire to repent to the One Who neither sleeps nor is heedless (of anything that happens).

The Reality Of Our Existence

The diversions of this world are often so enticing that those who are enjoying them do not see life for what it really is. That is why it is so rare, and actually nice when it happens, to see a ruler or king who perceives the reality of life.

Al-Asma'i reported that the ruler Ar-Rashid once ordered for many delicacies to be prepared for him. He wanted to have a nice party for himself, so he had a hall decorated for him, and he invited the famous poet Abul-'Atâhiyyah.

When the party had begun, Ar-Rashid looked at Abul-'Atâhiyyah and said, "Describe the pleasures of the world that we are enjoying." It was often the case that kings and rulers requested poets to compose impromptu verses for them. Abul-'Atâhiyyah began thus:

Live in comfort as long as you please,

Under the shades of high and wonderful castles.

"Wonderful, wonderful. Please continue," said Ar-Rashid.

Abul-'Atâhiyyah continued:

All that you desire is brought to you

Quickly, both in the morning and in the evening.

"Wonderful, wonderful," chimed in Ar-Rashid. "Please continue."

He resumed thus:

> Then when the souls are parting,
>
> Through the breast with a croaking sound,
>
> It is then that one comes to know:
>
> I have lived nothing but a life of deception.

Ar-Rashid began to weep profusely, and some of those who were present looked reproachfully at Abul-'Atâhiyyah and said, "The Leader of the Believers has invited you here to make him happy, yet all that you have succeeded in doing is making him sad!"

"Leave him alone," said Ar-Rashid with a sigh. "He simply noticed that we were in a state of blindness, and disliked adding to it with even more blindness."

---------- ❖ ❖ ❖ ----------

Can Even I Repent?

As Al-Hasan Al-Basri was riding away from the funeral of Abu Rajâ' Al-'Utâridi on his mule, Al-Farazdaq rode alongside him on his prized camel. Pointing towards the people who attended the funeral, Al-Farazdaq turned to Al-Hasan and said, "O Abu Sa'id, do you know what these people are saying? They are saying, 'Here goes the best *Shaikh* in Basrah (i.e., Al-Hasan), and here goes the most evil *Shaikh* of Al-Basrah (i.e., Al-Farazdaq).'" They vilified Al-Farazdaq because he had wrongfully accused chaste women of perpetrating lewd and wicked crimes.

"Then they are not telling the truth," said Al-Hasan, whose words probably took Al-Farazdaq by surprise, for Al-Farazdaq was well acquainted with his own misdeeds. Al-Hasan continued: "There are many *Shaikhs* (*Shaikh* here meaning old man, and not religious scholar) in Basrah who associate partners with Allâh in worship, and so they are more evil than Al-Farazdaq. And there are many *Shaikhs* in Basrah who own all but two tattered garments and are not given any attention by the people, but if they were to make an oath by Allâh, Allâh would cause it to be fulfilled for them; and so these are better than Al-Hasan." Al-Hasan then turned to Al-Farazdaq and said, "O Abu Firâs (i.e., Al-Farazdaq), what have you prepared for this day (i.e., death)?"

"The testimony that none has the right to be worshiped

except Allâh, a testimony that I have believed in for 80 years now," said Al-Farazdaq. "O Abu Sa'id, can even I repent?"

"Yes, by Allâh," said Al-Hasan.

"O Abu Sa'id, what should I do about wrongfully accusing chaste women?" asked Al-Farazdaq.

"Repent immediately and make a solid oath to Allâh that you will never do it again," said Al-Hasan.

"Then indeed, I make a solid oath to Allâh that I will never again wrongfully accuse any chaste woman," said Al-Farazdaq.

---------- ❖ ❖ ❖ ----------

It Was Because Of Their Repentance That They Were Saved

When we invoke Allâh (ﷺ) for help, we may refer to good deeds that we had previously performed sincerely for Allâh, thus increasing the likelihood of our repentance and supplications being answered. This point is clearly illustrated in the following narration, which is reported in *Al-Bukhâri*.

«بَيْنَمَا ثَلَاثَةُ نَفَرٍ يَمْشُونَ أَخَذَهُمُ المَطَرُ فَأَوَوْا إِلَى غَارٍ فِي جَبَلٍ، فَانْحَطَّتْ عَلَى فَمِ غَارِهِمْ صَخْرَةٌ مِنَ الجَبَلِ فَانْطَبَقَتْ عَلَيْهِمْ، فَقَالَ بَعْضُهُمْ لِبَعْضٍ: انْظُرُوا أَعْمَالًا عَمِلْتُمُوهَا صَالِحَةً لِلهِ فَادْعُوا اللهَ بِها لَعَلَّهُ يُفَرِّجُها عَنْكُمْ، قَالَ أَحَدُهُمْ: اللَّهُمَّ إِنَّهُ كَانَ لِي وَالِدَانِ شَيْخَانِ كَبِيرَانِ، وَلِي صِبْيَةٌ صِغَارٌ كُنْتُ أَرْعَىٰ عَلَيْهِمْ، فَإِذَا رُحْتُ عَلَيْهِمْ حَلَبْتُ فَبَدَأْتُ بِوَالِدَيَّ أَسْقِيهِمَا قَبْلَ بَنِيَّ، وَإِنِّي اسْتَأْخَرْتُ ذَاتَ يَوْمٍ وَلَمْ آتِ حَتَّى أَمْسَيْتُ فَوَجَدْتُهُمَا نَامَا، فَحَلَبْتُ كَمَا كُنْتُ أَحْلُبُ فَقُمْتُ عِنْدَ رُؤُوسِهِمَا، أَكْرَهُ أَنْ أُوقِظَهُمَا وَأَكْرَهُ أَنْ أَسْقِيَ الصِّبْيَةَ، وَالصِّبْيَةُ يَتَضَاغَوْنَ عِنْدَ قَدَمَيَّ حَتَّى طَلَعَ الفَجْرُ، فَإِنْ كُنْتَ تَعْلَمُ أَنِّي فَعَلْتُهُ ابْتِغَاءَ وَجْهِكَ فَافْرُجْ لَنَا فَرْجَةً نَرَى مِنها السَّمَاءَ، فَفَرَجَ اللهُ فَرَأَوُا السَّمَاءَ. وَقَالَ الآخَرُ: اللَّهُمَّ إِنَّها كَانَتْ لِي بِنْتُ عَمٍّ أَحْبَبْتُها كَأَشَدِّ مَا يُحِبُّ الرِّجَالُ النِّسَاءَ فَطَلَبْتُ مِنها فَأَبَتْ عَلَيَّ حَتَّى آتِيَها

بِمِائَةِ دِينَارٍ، فَبَغَيْتُ حَتَّى جَمَعْتُهَا، فَلَمَّا وَقَعْتُ بَيْنَ رِجْلَيْهَا قَالَتْ:
يَا عَبْدَ اللهِ، اتَّقِ اللهَ وَلَا تَفْتَحِ الْخَاتَمَ إِلَّا بِحَقِّهِ، فَقُمْتُ، فإنْ كُنْتَ
تَعْلَمُ أَنِّي فَعَلْتُهُ ابْتِغَاءَ وَجْهِكَ فَافْرُجْ عَنَّا فَرْجَةً، فَفَرَجَ. وَقَالَ
الثَّالِثُ: اللَّهُمَّ إِنِّي اسْتَأْجَرْتُ أَجِيرًا بِفَرَقِ أَرُزٍّ، فَلَمَّا قَضَى عَمَلَهُ
قَالَ: أَعْطِنِي حَقِّي، فَعَرَضْتُ عَلَيْهِ فَرَغِبَ عَنْهُ، فَلَمْ أَزَلْ أَزْرَعُهُ
حَتَّى جَمَعْتُ مِنْهُ بَقَرًا وَرُعَاتَهَا، فَجَاءَنِي فَقَالَ: اتَّقِ اللهَ، فَقُلْتُ:
اذْهَبْ إِلَى ذٰلِكَ الْبَقَرِ وَرُعَاتِها فَخُذْ، فَقَالَ: اتَّقِ اللهَ وَلا تَسْتَهْزِئْ
بِي، فَقَالَ: إِنِّي لَا أَسْتَهْزِئُ بِكَ، فَخُذْ، فَأَخَذَهُ، فإنْ كُنْتَ تَعْلَمُ أَنِّي
فَعَلْتُ ذٰلِكَ ابْتِغَاءَ وَجْهِكَ فَافْرُجْ مَا بَقِيَ، فَفَرَجَ اللهُ».

Narrated 'Abdullāh bin 'Umar ﷺ: The Prophet ﷺ said,
"While three men were walking, it started raining and
they took shelter (refuge) in a cave in a mountain. A big
rock rolled down from the mountain and closed the mouth
of the cave. They said to each other, 'Think of good deeds
which you did for Allāh's sake only, and invoke Allāh by
giving reference to those deeds so that He may remove this
rock from you.' One of them said, 'O Allāh! I had old
parents and small children and I used to graze the sheep
for them. On my return to them in the evening, I used to
milk (the sheep) and start providing my parents first of all
before my children. One day I was delayed and came late
at night and found my parents sleeping. I milked (the
sheep) as usual and stood by their heads. I hated to wake
them up and disliked to give milk to my children before
them, although my children were weeping (because of
hunger) at my feet till the day dawned. O Allāh! If I did
this for Your sake only, kindly remove the rock so that we

could see the sky through it.' So, Allāh removed the rock a
little and they saw the sky. The second man said, 'O
Allāh! I was in love with a cousin of mine like the deepest
love a man may have for a woman. I wanted to outrage her
chastity but she refused unless I gave her one-hundred
Dīnār. So, I struggled to collect that amount. And when I
sat between her legs, she said: O Allāh's slave! Be afraid of
Allāh and do not deflower me except rightfully (by legal
marriage). So, I got up. O Allāh! If I did it for Your sake
only, please remove the rock.' The rock shifted a little
more. Then the third man said, 'O Allāh! I employed a
labourer for a Faraq of rice and when he finished his job
and demanded his right, I presented it to him, but he
refused to take it. So, I sowed the rice many time till I
gathered cows and their shepherd (from the yield). (Then
after some time) he came and said to me: Fear Allāh (and
give me my right). I said: Go and take those cows and the
shepherd. He said: Be afraid of Allāh! Don't mock at me. I
said: I am not mocking at you. Take (all that). So, he took
all that. O Allāh! If I did that for Your sake only, please
remove the rest of the rock.' So, Allāh removed the
rock.''[1]

---------- ❖ ❖ ❖ ----------

---

[1] *Al-Bukhari*: 2333, Muslim 2743.

The Repentance Of
Ka'b bin Mâlik (رضي الله عنه)

When the Messenger of Allâh (ﷺ) resolved to go to Tabûk in order to face the Romans, he (ﷺ) ordered all of his Companions to make preparations for the expedition. Almost everyone went. Some who stayed behind were either too weak or too poor to be able to afford the journey; others remained behind because they were hypocrites; and there were three particular Companions (رضي الله عنهم) that remained behind, despite the fact that they were neither weak nor guilty of being hypocrites. One of these three was Ka'b bin Mâlik (رضي الله عنه).

Although Ka'b (رضي الله عنه) was a sincere Muslim, he continued to procrastinate until it became too late: the Muslims had left for the expedition, and the only people he saw when he went out into the marketplace were weak, sick, or poor Muslims who were not able to make the journey; as well as people – slightly more than eighty in total – who stayed behind without any sound excuse.

When the Muslims returned from the expedition, Ka'b) and his two companions رضي الله عنهم were boycotted: No one was allowed to speak to or greet them. Of course, by now Ka'b (رضي الله عنه) realized his error and felt a great deal of remorse. The entire earth, despite its wideness, felt constricted for him. Feeling sad and forlorn, Ka'b (رضي الله عنه) would weep uncontrollably as he asked Allâh (ﷻ) to forgive him. To be sure, his repentance was sincere, for Allâh (ﷻ) then revealed this Verse, informing the Muslims that He (ﷻ) had accepted the repentance of Ka'b and his two companions (ﷺ):

﴿لَّقَد تَّابَ ٱللَّهُ عَلَى ٱلنَّبِيِّ وَٱلْمُهَاجِرِينَ وَٱلْأَنصَارِ ٱلَّذِينَ ٱتَّبَعُوهُ فِى سَاعَةِ ٱلْعُسْرَةِ مِنۢ بَعْدِ مَا كَادَ يَزِيغُ قُلُوبُ فَرِيقٍ مِّنْهُمْ ثُمَّ تَابَ عَلَيْهِمْ إِنَّهُ بِهِمْ رَءُوفٌ رَّحِيمٌ ۝﴾

"Allâh has forgiven the Prophet (ﷺ), the Muhâjirûn (Muslim emigrants who left their homes and came to Al-Madinah) and the Ansâr (Muslims of Al-Madinah) who followed him [Muhammad (ﷺ)] in the times of distress (Tabûk expedition, etc.), after the hearts of a party of them had nearly deviated (from the Right Path), but He accepted their repentance. Certainly, He is unto them full of Kindness, Most Merciful."[1]

--------- ❖ ❖ ❖ ---------

---

[1] *Qur'ân* 9:117.

Repent Throughout The Day

Talq bin Habib said, "Indeed, the rights of Allâh (ﷺ) are too great for His slaves to be able to fulfill them. And indeed, His favors and blessings are too many for them to be able to enumerate them. Then (the only way to safety) is for you to wake up every morning and repent for your sins; and to go bed every night and repent for your sins."

---------- ❖ ❖ ❖ ----------

When I Die...

The following story is mentioned in an authentic *Hadîth* that is narrated by Abu Hurairah (ﷺ):

«قَالَ رَجُلٌ - لَمْ يَعْمَلْ حَسَنَةً قَطُّ - لِأَهْلِهِ: إِذَا مَاتَ فَحَرِّقُوهُ ثُمَّ اذْرُوا نِصْفَهُ فِي الْبَرِّ وَنِصْفَهُ فِي الْبَحْرِ. فَوَاللهِ! لَئِنْ قَدَرَ اللهُ عَلَيْهِ لِيُعَذِّبَنَّهُ عَذَابًا لَا يُعَذِّبُهُ أَحَدًا مِنَ الْعَالَمِينَ، فَلَمَّا مَاتَ الرَّجُلُ فَعَلُوا مَا أَمَرَهُمْ، فَأَمَرَ اللهُ الْبَرَّ فَجَمَعَ مَا فِيهِ، وَأَمَرَ الْبَحْرَ فَجَمَعَ مَا فِيهِ، ثُمَّ قَالَ: لِمَ فَعَلْتَ هَذَا؟ قَالَ: مِنْ خَشْيَتِكَ يَارَبِّ! وَأَنْتَ أَعْلَمُ، فَغَفَرَ اللهُ لَهُ»

"A man who had never performed a good deed throughout his life gave these instructions to his family: When I die, burn me and scatter half of my remains on land, and the other half in the sea. For by Allâh, if Allâh is able to get me, He will punish me as He punishes no one else from the entire creation!

"When he died, his family followed his instructions to the letter. Allâh (ﷺ) then ordered the land to gather together his remains that were scattered on it, and the sea to gather together his remains that were scattered in it. Then when the man was brought together again, Allâh (ﷺ) asked him

why he did what he did. He said, "From fear of You, O my Lord! And You know best (as to what was in my heart)." Allâh (ﷻ) then forgave him."[1]

---------- ❖ ❖ ❖ ----------

---
[1] *Al-Bukhari*: 7506 and *Muslim*: 2756.

The Sinner Who Constantly Repents

Abu Ja'far Al-Bâqir narrated that his father 'Ali bin Al-Husain said, "Indeed, Allâh (ﷻ) loves the sinner who constantly repents."

Prevention Is The Best Remedy

To be sure, every single one of us is a sinner, and the best among us are those who constantly repent. But it is nonetheless dangerous for one sin on purpose with the intention of repenting later on, for perhaps he might not live long enough to repent, or perhaps he will somehow – because of his sin and his brazenness in performing it – be prevented from repenting.

Al-Hasan once said, "O son of Adam, to abstain from a sin is easier for you than curing it later on through repentance. How can you be sure that you will not perpetrate a deed so grave in its wickedness that the door of repentance will be closed before you..."

---------- ❖ ❖ ❖ ----------

Whoever Wants To Repent...

When in the company of others, one cannot easily contemplate his situation in life, for he will be too conscious of those around him to engage in sincere introspection. It is only when one is alone that he can think clearly enough to assess his deeds and to repent his misdeeds. Ibrâhim bin Adham once said, "Whoever wants to repent, then let him come out of darkness, and let him forsake the company of people. Otherwise, he will.

---------- ❖ ❖ ❖ ----------

He (ﷺ) Brought Me To Them So That I Can Reform My Character

Al-Fudail bin 'Iyâd was famous for his piety and worship, but he was not always a practicing Muslim. In his early years, Al-Fudail was an infamous highway robber; he would prowl in the night for victims on the road from Abiward to Sarakhs. Between these two cities was a small village, in which lived a girl that Al-Fudail was in love with. One night, out of desperation to be with her, Al-Fudail climbed the wall of her home. As he was climbing over it, he heard someone recite thisVerse of the Qur'ân:

﴿أَلَمْ يَأْنِ لِلَّذِينَ ءَامَنُوٓاْ أَن تَخْشَعَ قُلُوبُهُمْ لِذِكْرِ ٱللَّهِ﴾

"Has not the time come for the hearts of those who believe (in the Oneness of Allâh – Islamic Monotheism) to be affected by Allâh's Reminder (this Qur'ân)."[1]

This was the moment in which Fudail changed; he answered, "O my Lord, the time has indeed come (for me to be affect by Allâh's Reminder)." He returned from whence he came and sought refuge near a traveling party on the main road. They were busily engaged in a serious discussion. Fudail heard one of them say, "Let us continue our journey now." Another answered, "No, not until the morning, for Fudail is lurking on the road somewhere out there, just waiting to rob us." Having heard the entire conversation, Al-Fudail thought to himself: "I go around in the night to sin, while a group of Muslims remains here because they fear me. Indeed, I feel that Allâh (ﷻ) has brought me here to them only so that I can reform my character. O Allâh, I indeed repent to You..."

---------- ❖ ❖ ❖ ----------

---

[1] *Qur'ân* 57:16.

Old Age

Abu Hâmid Al-Ghazâli reported this story:

There was a young man among the Children of Israel who worshiped Allâh (ﷻ) for twenty years. He then disobeyed Allâh (ﷻ) for twenty years. Then, one day, looking in the mirror, he noticed the whiteness of his beard and was taken aback by what he saw. He said, "O my Lord, I had obeyed you for twenty years, and I then disobeyed you for twenty years. Now if I return to You, will You accept me." Though he could not see anyone, he heard a caller say, "You loved Us, and We loved you. You (then) left Us, and so We left you. You disobeyed Us, and so We gave you respite. And if you return to Us, We will accept you."

---------- ❖ ❖ ❖ ----------

The Hallmarks Of
A Sincere Repentance

Shaqiq said: "Weeping over past (misdeeds), being afraid of perpetrating a sin again, forsaking the company of evildoers, and adhering to the company of the righteous – these are the hallmarks of a (sincere) repentance."

---------- ❖ ❖ ❖ ----------

My Lord, Here Is My Forelock
In Your Hand

As two servants of the ruler, An-Nâsir, were talking to one another, one of them said, "I wonder what the ruler is doing today?" The other said, "I never saw him more afraid and sincere than he is today. He is by himself, wearing coarse clothing and sitting down on dirt. He is crying out loud and acknowledging his sins. I heard him say, 'My Lord, here is my forelock in Your Hand, if You are to punish the people, and You are All-Wise and All-

Just, then how will I, with all of my (sins), escape Your (punishment)?'''

At that moment, Mundhir bin Sa'id was passing by, and he heard what the ruler's servant said. Mundhir looked at him and said, 'O young servant, wear a raincoat back with you, for if the mighty one on earth becomes fearful (of Allâh's punishment), then the All-Mighty One in the heavens will have mercy (on His slaves and bless them with rain and sustenance).''

---------- ❖ ❖ ❖ ----------

Constantly Sinning And Constantly Repenting

Abu Hurairah (رضي الله عنه) narrated that the Prophet (صلى الله عليه وسلم) said:

«أَذْنَبَ عَبْدٌ ذَنْبًا فَقَالَ: اللَّهُمَّ! اغْفِرْ لِي ذَنْبِي فَقَالَ تَبَارَكَ وَتَعَالَى: عَبْدِي أَذْنَبَ ذَنْبًا فَعَلِمَ أَنَّ لَهُ رَبًّا يَغْفِرُ الذَّنْبَ، وَيَأْخُذُ بِالذَّنْبِ، ثُمَّ عَادَ فَأَذْنَبَ فَقَالَ: أَيْ رَبِّ! اغْفِرْ لِي ذَنْبِي، فَقَالَ تَبَارَكَ وَتَعَالَى: عَبْدِي أَذْنَبَ ذَنْبًا فَعَلِمَ أَنَّ لَهُ رَبًّا يَغْفِرُ الذَّنْبَ، وَيَأْخُذُ بِالذَّنْبِ، ثُمَّ عَادَ فَأَذْنَبَ فَقَالَ: أَيْ رَبِّ، اغْفِرْ لِي ذَنْبِي، فَقَالَ تَبَارَكَ وَتَعَالَى: أَذْنَبَ عَبْدِي ذَنْبًا فَعَلِمَ أَنَّ لَهُ رَبًّا يَغْفِرُ الذَّنْبَ، وَيَأْخُذُ بِالذَّنْبِ، اعْمَلْ مَا شِئْتَ فَقَدْ غَفَرْتُ لَكَ»

"A slave (of Allâh) sinned and then said, 'O Allâh, forgive me my sin.' Allâh, Most Blessed and Most High, said, 'My slave perpetrated a sin, and he knew that he has a Lord Who forgives sins and punishes (people) for (their) sins.' That (slave of Allâh) then returned and sinned again, after which he said, 'My Lord! Forgive me my sin.' Allâh, Most Blessed and Most High, said, 'My slave perpetrated a sin, and he knew that he has a Lord Who forgives sins and punishes (people) for (their) sins.' He then returned and sinned again, after which he said, 'My Lord, forgive me my sin.' Allâh, Most Blessed and Most High, said, 'My slave perpetrated a sin, and he knew that he has a Lord Who forgives sins and punishes (people) for

(their) sins. Do as you wish, for I have indeed forgiven you (i.e., as long as you repent sincerely and feel remorseful for having sinned, I will continue to forgive you)."[1]

---------- ❖ ❖ ❖ ----------

The Advice Of Khidr (ﷺ)

Abu Hâmid Al-Ghazâli reported that Mûsa (ﷺ) asked Khidr (ﷺ) to advise him. Khidr said:

"Be someone who constantly smiles, and not someone who is constantly angry, be someone who benefits others, and not someone who harms others. Refrain from (false or useless) argumentation. Do not walk around without purpose. Do not laugh without wonderment (i.e., without a reason). Do not disparage wrongdoers by mentioning their mistakes to them. And cry over your misdeeds, O son of 'Imrân."

---------- ❖ ❖ ❖ ----------

The Advice Of Al-Hasan

Al-Hasan once wrote the following short letter to 'Umar bin 'Abdul-'Aziz:

"Fear what Allâh told you to fear. Take what is in your hands, and use it for what is to come (i.e., the Hereafter). At the moment of death, sure news will come to you and peace."

'Umar wrote back, asking Al-Hasan to advise him some more. This is the letter that Al-Hasan wrote back:

"Indeed the terror (of the Day of Resurrection) is greater (that you might think). Indeed, frightful matters are near at hand. You will have to face all of that, either by facing it all and being saved, or by facing it all and being destroyed. Know that he who takes account of his own deeds will succeed, and that he who is negligent in this regard will fail. Whoever looks at the outcomes of his actions will be saved, while he who obeys his desires will be misguided. Whoever is patient and forbearing will gain profits. Whoever remains awake and vigilant (regarding his deeds) will be safe; whoever is safe, reflects; whoever reflects, sees; whoever sees, understands; and whoever understands, knows. Then if you slip, return (and repent). And when you are remorseful, then refrain (from returning to your sin). When you are ignorant, ask. And when you are angry, restrain your anger."

The Covering Of Sins

'Abdullah bin Mas'ûd (ﷺ) narrated that a man once kissed a woman who was unlawful to him, then went to the Prophet (ﷺ), and informed him of what had happened. This Verse was then revealed:

﴿وَأَقِمِ ٱلصَّلَوٰةَ طَرَفِيِ ٱلنَّهَارِ وَزُلَفًا مِّنَ ٱلَّيۡلِ إِنَّ ٱلۡحَسَنَٰتِ يُذۡهِبۡنَ ٱلسَّيِّئَاتِ ذَٰلِكَ ذِكۡرَىٰ لِلذَّٰكِرِينَ ۝﴾

"And perform As-Salât (Iqâmatas-Salat), at the two ends of the day and in some hours of the night [i.e., the five compulsory Salât (prayer)]. Verily, the good deeds remove the evil deeds (i.e., small sins). That is a reminder (an advice) for the mindful (those who accept advice)."[1]

The man asked, "O Messenger of Allâh, is this for me?" "It is for anyone from my nation who applies it," answered the Prophet (ﷺ).

---------- ❖ ❖ ❖ ----------

---
[1] *Qur'ân* 11:114.

A Similar Text To The Last One

'Abdullah (﷽) narrated that a man went to the Prophet (ﷺ) and said, "O Messenger of Allâh! I have indeed been with a woman (i.e., I was fondling her) at the furthest end of Al-Madinah; I had her without touching her (i.e., without having sexual intercourse with her). Now here I am, so issue whatever judgment you please against me." 'Umar (﷽) said to the man, "Allâh would have indeed covered you (i.e., covered your sin), had you covered yourself (i.e., had you not told anyone about your sin, but instead repented in secret)." Meanwhile, the Prophet (ﷺ) said nothing. The man then stood up and left. The Prophet (ﷺ) sent a messenger to go after him and to recite this Verse to him:

﴿وَأَقِمِ ٱلصَّلَوٰةَ طَرَفِيِ ٱلنَّهَارِ وَزُلَفًا مِّنَ ٱلَّيْلِ إِنَّ ٱلْحَسَنَٰتِ يُذْهِبْنَ ٱلسَّيِّئَاتِ ذَٰلِكَ ذِكْرَىٰ لِلذَّٰكِرِينَ ١١٤﴾

"And perform As-Salat (Iqâmatas-Salât), at the two ends of the day and in some hours of the night [i.e., the five compulsory Salât (prayer)]. Verily, the good deeds remove the evil deeds (i.e., small sins). That is a reminder (an advice) for the mindful (those who accept advice)."[1]

"O Prophet of Allâh, is this particular to him?" asked a man who was present.

"Rather, it is for all people," answered the Prophet (ﷺ).

---

[1] *Qur'ân* 11:114.

You Have Indeed Been Forgiven

Anas (☻) narrated that a man went to the Prophet (ﷺ) and said, "O Messenger of Allâh, I have perpetrated a sin for which there is a prescribed punishment, so apply it on me." As it was time for the congregational prayer, the man then stayed to pray with the Messenger of Allâh (ﷺ). When the prayer was finished, the man went to the Prophet (ﷺ) and repeated what he had said earlier: "O Messenger of Allâh, I have perpetrated a sin for which there is a prescribed punishment, so apply on me that which is in the Book of Allâh."

The Prophet (ﷺ) asked:

«هَلْ حَضَرْتَ الصَّلَاةَ مَعَنَا؟»

"Did you perform prayer with us?"

"Yes," said the man.

The Prophet said (ﷺ):

«قَدْ غُفِرَ لَكَ»

"Then you have indeed been forgiven."[1]

---------- ❖ ❖ ❖ ----------

---
[1] *Al-Bukhari*: 6823 and *Muslim*: 2764.

A Similar Text To The Previous One

Abu Umâmah (مع) said, "While we were seated with the Messenger of Allâh (ﷺ) in the *Masjid*, a man came and said, 'O Messenger of Allâh, I have indeed perpetrated a sin for which there is a prescribed punishment, so apply it (the punishment) on me.'" After the man finished speaking, the Prophet (ﷺ) remained silent, and the prayer then commenced.

Abu Umâmah continued: "Afterwards, the man followed the Messenger of Allâh (ﷺ) as he left, and I too followed the Messenger of Allâh (ﷺ), wanting to see what response he would give to the man. When the man caught up to the Messenger of Allâh (ﷺ), he said, 'O Messenger of Allâh, I have indeed perpetrated a sin for which there is a prescribed punishment, so apply it on me.' The Messenger of Allâh (ﷺ) said to him:

«أَرَأَيْتَ حِينَ خَرَجْتَ مِنْ بَيْتِكَ، أَلَيْسَ قَدْ تَوَضَّأْتَ فَأَحْسَنْتَ الْوُضُوءَ؟!»

'Remember when you left your home: did you not perform ablution and perform it well?'

'Yes, O Messenger of Allâh,' said the man. 'Then you attended the prayer with us?' asked the Prophet (ﷺ). 'Yes, O Messenger of Allâh,' answered the man. The Messenger of Allâh (ﷺ) then said:

«فَإِنَّ اللَّهَ قَدْ غَفَرَ لَكَ حَدَّكَ - أَوْ قَالَ - ذَنْبَكَ»

*'Then Allâh has indeed forgiven your Hadd (punishment)
(or he (ﷺ) said, 'forgiven your sin').'*[1]

---------- ❖ ❖ ❖ ----------

[1] *Muslim*: 2765 and *Abu Dawud*: 4381.

Important Points Concerning Repentance That We Must Understand

From the preceding narrations we should derive an appreciation for the greatness of our religion and for the mercy of Allâh (﷾), Who is the Most Merciful of the merciful ones. But still, as slaves of Allâh (﷾), we must do our part; we must take certain steps to deserve forgiveness from Allâh (﷾).

First, we must desist from the sin for which we are guilty. Second, we must sincerely feel regret for having perpetrated that sin, and at the same time we must hasten to ask forgiveness from Allâh (﷾). Third, we must make a firm resolve never to return to that sin. Fourth, we must hasten to perform good deeds, for by the permission of Allâh (﷾), it is always the case that good deeds atone for and remove evil deeds.

Abu Sa'id Al-Khudri (﷜) narrated that he heard the Messenger of Allâh (ﷺ) say:

«إِنَّ إِبْلِيسَ قَالَ لِرَبِّهِ عَزَّ وَجَلَّ: بِعِزَّتِكَ وَجَلَالِكَ! لَا أَبْرَحُ أُغْوِي بَنِي آدَمَ مَا دَامَتِ الْأَرْوَاحُ فِيهِمْ، قَالَ اللهُ عَزَّ وَجَلَّ: فَبِعِزَّتِي وَجَلَالِي! لَا أَبْرَحُ أَغْفِرُ لَهُمْ مَا اسْتَغْفَرُونِي»

"Indeed, Iblis (the Devil) said to his Lord 'Azza wa-Jall (the Possessor of might and majesty), 'By Your Might and Majesty, I will continue to tempt and misguide the children of Adam as long as they have souls in them.

Allâh ﷺ said:

"Then by My Might and Majesty, I will continue to forgive them as long as they ask Me to forgive them."[1]

---------- ❖ ❖ ❖ ----------

---

[1] *Al-Musnad* 3/29.

Repentance Is Sweet

A tyrant ruler once left his castle to walk around the streets of his realm in order to enjoy himself. As he was walking, he came across a number of gardens and decided to enter one of them. After spending a short while looking at the garden's beautiful trees, he became thirsty, and so he asked the owner of the garden, who was standing nearby, for a drink. The owner told him that though there was no water nearby, the ruler was free to take a pomegranate and quench his thirst by eating it. The ruler agreed, and when he took his first bite from the pomegranate that was given to him, he was amazed to see how wonderfully, and almost unnaturally, sweet it was. He said to himself: "This pomegranate is indeed wonderful." He decided to evict the owner and take possession of the garden. But first he wanted to make sure that all of the pomegranates of the garden were equally wonderful and sweet, and so he asked for another one. When he began to eat a second pomegranate, he was shocked to see that it was very bitter and foul tasting.

He asked the owner if it was from same tree as the first pomegranate. "Yes," said the owner.

"Then how come it is not as sweet as the first?" inquired

the ruler.

"O leader, perhaps you intended to do some evil, which caused its taste to change," said the righteous garden owner.

"By Allâh, the man has spoken the truth," thought the ruler. After repenting from his intention to usurp the garden, the ruler decided that he wanted to enjoy another pomegranate, and so he asked for one. When he tasted it, he was amazed to see that it was even sweeter than the first one he had eaten. What is more, it was from the very same tree.

For the one who repents, my beloved readers, life is always sweet and wonderful. Allâh (ﷻ) said:

$$﴿وَأَنِ ٱسْتَغْفِرُوا۟ رَبَّكُمْ ثُمَّ تُوبُوٓا۟ إِلَيْهِ يُمَتِّعْكُم مَّتَـٰعًا حَسَنًا إِلَىٰٓ أَجَلٍ مُّسَمًّى وَيُؤْتِ كُلَّ ذِى فَضْلٍ فَضْلَهُۥٓ﴾$$

"And (commanding you): "Seek the forgiveness of your Lord, and turn to Him in repentance, that He may grant you good enjoyment, for a term appointed, and bestow His abounding Grace to every owner of grace (i.e., the one who helps and serves needy and deserving, physically and with his wealth, and even with good words)."[1]

---------- ❖ ❖ ❖ ----------

---

[1] *Qur'ân* 11:3.

It Is Indeed You Who Are The Rider, And I Who Am The Foot-Traveler

One year, Ibrâhim bin Adham decided to perform *Hajj* on foot, walking not just from one place to another in Makkah, but also to and from his homeland, which meant a long and arduous trek. As he was leaving his homeland, a man riding on a camel passed by and said, "O Ibn Adham, where are you going?"

"I am going to perform *Hajj*, if Allâh wills," said Ibrâhim.

"Then where is your mount, Ibn Adham, for the journey is long?" asked the man.

"I have many mounts that I ride upon, though you cannot see them," said Ibrâhim.

"What?" asked the man, not comprehending Ibrâhim's meaning.

"If I am afflicted with a calamity, I ride on the mount (figuratively, of course) of patience (for just as a mount takes a person from one place to another, patience takes one to safety in the Hereafter). If I am given a blessing, I ride on the mount of thankfulness. If something that is decreed (and that is difficult to bear) happens to me, I ride on the mount of contentment. And when my soul invites me (to satisfy some lust or desire), I reflect on how the time I have left on earth is less than the time that has already gone by."

"You are indeed traveling by the command of Allâh," said the man. "Then by Allâh, it is you who are the rider, and I who am the foot-traveler."

---------- ❖ ❖ ❖ ----------

Then How Will You Withstand The Fire Of The Hereafter!

'Abdullah bin Marzûq, who was a close friend of the ruler Al-Mahdi, was drunk one day and consequently missed the congregational prayer. His female servant came to him with a piece of burning wood and placed it on his leg. Needless to say he jumped up to with a hideous expression of pain on his face.

"If you cannot withstand the fire of the earth, then how will you withstand the Fire of the Hereafter (which is about 70 times more intense than the fire of this world)?" asked the servant.

Having understood the point of the painful lesson, 'Abdullâh bin Marzûq repented immediately. Thereafter, he performed his prayers on time and gave away a great deal that he owned for charity. After some time passed, Al-Fudail bin 'Iyâd and Ibn 'Uyaynah visited 'Abdullah bin Marzûq, and just by looking at him and at the furniture of his home, they noticed a drastic change in the man's lifestyle. Referring to his simple way of living, they asked, "No one forsakes something for Allâh, except that Allâh compensates him with something (equal or better); so what did Allâh compensate you with for the (worldly pleasures) that you abandoned?"

"Contentment for the situation I find myself to be in," said 'Abdullah bin Marzûq.

O Wretched Man!

There is an Israelite narration that mentions an interesting story of a fisherman who lived during the era of Mûsa (ﷺ). He was a poor fisherman and physically weak. One day, he lifted his fishing net and was surprised, not to mention somewhat thrilled, to see that he had caught an exceptionally large fish. He immediately went with it to the marketplace, intending to sell it and use the proceeds of the sale to buy things that his family desperately needed.

But before he could reach the marketplace, a huge, muscular man accosted him and, upon seeing the fish, tried to take it by force. The fisherman put up as much resistance as he could, but the other man raised a piece of wood he had in his hand and struck the fisherman with it on his head. While the fisherman was lying flat on the ground, writhing in pain, his attacker took off with the fish. As the helpless fisherman watched the man leave with his fish, he said, "O my Lord, you have made me weak, and him strong, so take my right from him quickly, for he has wronged me, and I do not want to patiently wait until the Hereafter (to exact retribution from him)."

When the wrongdoer returned to his home with the nice, large fish, he gave it to his wife and ordered her to barbecue it for him. After she finished cooking it, she placed it before him on the table. As the man was fingering his food, the fish closed its mouth on his finger.

The pain that resulted from the bite (that came from a dead fish!) was more than the man could bear; the pain was not merely temporary; it simply wouldn't go away. And so the man went to the doctor to complain about the unbearable pain in his finger. After he studied the man's hand, the doctor said, "The only cure is to cut off your finger, so that the pain doesn't spread to the rest of your hand."

The doctor then severed the man's finger, but to the man's utter dismay, the pain he had felt in his finger, he now felt in his hand. The doctor said that he would have to cut his hand off, so as to prevent the pain from spreading to his forearm. But as soon as the doctor severed the man's hand, the pain spread to his forearm. And this continued, until the doctor began to amputate other limbs. Writhing in pain, the man invoked Allâh (ﷻ) to help him.

One night, he saw a dream, in which someone said to him, "O wretched person, for how long will you have your body parts severed? Go to your adversary, whom you wronged, and try to gain his pardon." Waking up with a start, the man knew that the person in his dream was referring to the fisherman. He went to the city, searched for the fisherman, and upon finding him, pleaded with him to forgive him. He even gave the fisherman some money to recompense him for his stolen fish. Seeing that the man had truly repented for his misdeed, the fisherman forgave him. The man's pain immediately went away, and for the first time in many nights, he was able to enjoy a goodnight's sleep.

By Allâh, I Will Leap Up On
Them In Paradise

There is something common among the early Muslims from the *Muhâjirûn* and the *Ansâr*. Although some of them may have previously been staunch enemies of Islam, when they repented their *Shirk* and embraced Islam, they showed a level of sincerity that has remained unparalleled throughout history. One example is the noble Companion 'Amr bin Al-Jamûh (🙵), who at first resisted the Prophet's message, at a time when those around him in Al-Madinah, from the Aus and Khazraj, began to flock towards Islam.

Before migrating to Al-Madinah, the Prophet (ﷺ) sent Mus'ab bin 'Umair (🙵) to go there and teach its inhabitants about the religion of Islam. Mus'ab (🙵) was very successful in his early efforts, but then one day, 'Amr bin Al-Jamûh, chief of the Banu Salamah sub-tribe, sent for him with the message: "What is this that you have come to us with?"

"If you want to come to us, we will recite the Qur'ân for you," was the response he received. When 'Amr (🙵) and Mus'ab (🙵) were face to face, the latter recited 'Chapter Yûsuf' to him. Perhaps the Verses had an affect on 'Amr (🙵), but he was as of yet unwilling to renounce his religion or his idol, Manâf, which he worshiped and trusted. That is not to say that doubts did not begin to creep into his mind about the divinity of Manâf. As a test, he went to his idol, Manâf, and hung a sword around its neck, so that it could protect itself now that so many people – including his own family – shunned the worship of idols and called to the worship of the One True God – Allâh (ﷻ).

When he later returned to Manâf, he was shocked to see that the sword was missing, for unbeknownst to him, his family had taken the sword away. 'Amr (﴿) looked reproachfully at his idol and said, "Where is the sword, O Manâf. Even a she-goat is able to protect its backside." Despite Manâf's failure to protect itself, 'Amr (﴿) still made no firm resolve to accept Islam.

He turned to his family and said, "I am going to watch over my wealth (property or livestock), so take care of Manâf while I am gone." When he left, they took the idol, broke it, tied a dead dog around it, and threw it into an unused well.

"How are you?" 'Amr (﴿) asked his family when he returned from his errand.

"Fine," they said. "We have purified our house from filth."

"By Allâh, I think that you have done ill towards Manâf while I was gone," said 'Amr.

"There he is; go find him in the well," they said. He looked into the well and saw what his family had done with Manâf. Without delay, he summoned the members of his subtribe and said, "Do you not follow that which I follow?"

"Yes, you are our chief," they said.

"Then I make you bear witness that I indeed believe in what has been revealed to Muhammad."

Now let us move forward a few years to the Battle of Uhud, so that we can see the complete transformation of 'Amr's character. Shortly before the army of polytheists and the army of Muslims began the famous battle, the Messenger of Allâh (ﷺ) said to his Companions ﷺ: "Stand up to Paradise, the width of which is (equal to the distance of) the heavens and the earth, and it has been prepared for the *Muttaqûn* (the righteous ones)."

'Amr (ﷺ), who was physically crippled, struggled to get up and said, "By Allâh I will leap up on them (i.e., on these weak legs of mine) in Paradise." He (ﷺ) then continued to fight until he became martyred.

---------- ❖ ❖ ❖ ----------

Safety...Safety!

'Abdur-Rahmân bin Yazid said, "During military campaigns, I would rest (at night) in the same camp that 'Atâ' Al-Khurâsâni was staying in. At the beginning of every night, he would stick out his head from the inside of his tent and say, "O 'Abdur-Rahmân, O Hishim bin Al-Ghâz, O so-and-so – it is easier to fast during the day and stand for prayer during the night than to drink *As-Sadid* (boiling, festering water in the Hell-fire: refer to the Qur'ân 14: 16), to wear *Al-Hadid* (refer to the Qur'ân: 22: 21)

"And for them are hooked rods of iron (to punish them)", and to eat *Az-Zaqqûm* (refer to the Qur'ân 37: 62) "Is that (Paradise) better entertainment or the tree of *Zaqqûm* (a horrible tree in hell?" "(Then seek out) safety! ... (Then seek out) safety!"

---------- ❖ ❖ ❖ ----------

Silah

Silah, a righteous man who lived centuries ago, was once on a journey when he completely ran out of food. There had been a flood, and so there were many like him who were stranded and wandering about. He came across a man who was carrying bread on his shoulders, and so Silah accosted him and said, "Feed me."

"If you want," said the man, "But there is pork mixed into the bread." Although he was on the verge of dying, Silah left the man without taking any bread. Later on, he met another man and said, "Feed me."

"I have enough provision to last me a few days only," said the man. "If you take from it, then you will make me go hungry."

Silah moved on without taking any food from the man. Having continued his journey, Silah heard a sound behind him. He stopped, turned around, and headed towards the direction of the sound. When he reached the spot from which he thought he had heard the noise, he found a white cloth that was wrapped up. Unraveling the cloth, Silah found fresh dates inside and realized that he was saved from imminent starvation. It was not as great a surprise to find the fresh dates in that spot, as it was to find them at that time – for it wasn't even the season for fresh dates!

How Wuhaib Repented

Speaking about the reason for his repentance, Wuhaib bin Al-Ward said, "As I was standing in the heart of a valley, I felt a man's hand on the back of my shoulder. He said, 'O Wuhaib, fear Allâh for his ability over you, and be modest of Him for His nearness to you.' By the time I turned around, there was no one to be seen." That incident is what prompted Wuhaib to repent.

---------- ❖ ❖ ❖ ----------

The Blessing Of Repentance...
Or The Blessing Of Richness

A resident of Damascus, 'Ubaidah bin Muhâjir was a well-respected, and extremely rich, businessman, who one day decided to make a business trip to Azerbaijan. After a long day of travel, 'Ubaidah came across a pasture and a river that ran alongside it. After he had made camp and was resting, he heard the sound of someone praising Allâh (ﷻ).

Going to the source of the sound, 'Ubaidah came across a man who, attired in a garment made of straw, was resting in a ditch. After having extended greetings of peace to the man, 'Ubaidah inquired, "Who are you, O slave of Allâh?"

"A Muslim," answered the man.

"How difficult your circumstances seem to be," said 'Ubaidah.

"I lead a life that is replete with blessings," said the man.

"How can you say that when you are wearing not clothing, but a covering made of straw!" exclaimed 'Ubaidah.

"And why shouldn't I praise Allâh for creating me, for giving me good form, for causing me to be born and raised as a Muslim, for blessing me with sound health, and for covering that part of my body which I dislike mentioning? Who goes to sleep having greater blessings than these, all of which I enjoy?"

"May Allâh have mercy on you," said 'Ubaidah. "Will you not come back with me to my camp, for I have made camp beside the river?"

"Why?" the man asked.

"So that I can feed you and give you real clothing, making it unnecessary for you to wear straw."

"I have no need for any of that," said the man.

'Ubaidah later said, "I then left him and returned to my campsite. I later fell into contemplation, and the more I thought about my situation, the more I despised my life and even myself. Here I was, the richest man in Damascus, having no fear of anyone in Damascus having even nearly as much wealth as I had, yet I was going on a journey to make even more money. It was at that point that I said: O Allâh, I indeed repent to You for the evilness of my situation." 'Ubaidah thereafter turned away from the pursuit of acquiring wealth, and instead dedicated his life to repentance and worship.

---------- ❖ ❖ ❖ ----------

A Visit To The Graveyard

Once, when Maimûn bin Mihrân and 'Umar bin 'Abdul-'Aziz (&) were visiting the graveyard together, the latter began to cry, and turning towards the former, he said, "O Abu Ayyûb (i.e., Maimûn), these are the graves of my fathers from Banu Umayyah. When I see their graves now, it seems as if they never participated with the dwellers of the world in their pleasures and (enjoyment-filled) lives. Do you not see how they are inextricably beset by trials? The insects are feeding off of their bodies..." 'Umar (&) then began to weep until he fainted. When he regained consciousness, he said, "Let us go, for by Allâh, I do not know of anyone who is more blessed than he who comes to these graves, yet is saved from the punishment of Allâh!"

---------- ❖ ❖ ❖ ----------

The Repentance Of Nûh (Noah)(ﷺ)

First, let us read about the repentance of Nûh (Noah) (ﷺ), and then let us reflect on our own daily lives and on how we repent from our sins. Wuhaib bin Al-Ward reported that after Allâh (ﷻ) reproached Nûh (Noah) (ﷺ) in regards to his son, Nûh (Noah) (ﷺ) cried for 300 years. He cried so much that the constant tears became like streams flowing down his cheeks.

﴿قَالَ يَـٰنُوحُ إِنَّهُۥ لَيْسَ مِنْ أَهْلِكَ إِنَّهُۥ عَمَلٌ غَيْرُ صَـٰلِحٍ فَلَا تَسْـَٔلْنِ مَا لَيْسَ لَكَ بِهِۦ عِلْمٌ إِنِّىٓ أَعِظُكَ أَن تَكُونَ مِنَ ٱلْجَـٰهِلِينَ ٤٦﴾

"He said: "O Nûh (Noah)! Surely, he is not of your family; verily, his work is unrighteous, so ask not of Me that of which you have no knowledge! I admonish you, lest you be one of the ignorants."[1]

---------- ❖ ❖ ❖ ----------

---
[1] *Qur'ân* 11:46.

A Heavy Burden

There was once a devoted worshipper among the Children of Israel who owned nothing except for a robe made of wool and a water canteen, which he would use when he would go around offering thirsty people a drink of water. When he was on his deathbed, he said to his companions, "Indeed, all that I leave behind in terms of worldly things are my robe and my canteen. I cannot bear carrying them on the Day of Resurrection, so when I die, give them to the king, for he will be able to carry them along with all of his other worldly possessions."

When the worshipper died, his companions went to the king and told him what the worshipper had said before dying.

"This worshipper says that he will not be able to carry a mere robe and canteen!" exclaimed the king. "Then, on the Day of Resurrection, how will I be able to carry all of the worldly things that I have in my possession?" He accepted the robe and wore it. Then, taking the canteen in his hand, he left his kingdom and began a new life that was devoted to the worship of Allâh (ﷻ) and to the service of His creation: he, like the previous owner of the canteen, went around serving thirsty people water.

---------- ❖ ❖ ❖ ----------

The Ranking Of A Person Who Repents

Bakr bin 'Abdullâh Al-Muzani is the narrator of this story: There was once a butcher who fell in love with the daughter of one of his neighbors. One day, the girl's parents sent her on an errand to a neighboring town. Seeing that she was alone, the butcher followed her until she reached a secluded place, where he made his presence known to her. When he tried to seduce her, the girl said, "Do not do so! Indeed, I love you even more than you love me, but I fear Allâh." The butcher's jaws dropped as he said in self-reproach, "You fear Allâh, and I don't!" He left her alone and repented for his evil intentions.

On his way back, he became extremely thirsty. He soon came across a Prophet (ﷺ) from the Prophets of the Children of Israel. Noticing the disconcerted and pained expression on the butcher's face, the Prophet (ﷺ) asked, "What is the matter with you?"

"Extreme thirst," said the butcher.

"Let us go and supplicate to Allâh (for rain)."

"I have no good deed (that makes my supplication worthy of being answered)," said the butcher.

"Then let me invoke Allâh while you say, '*Âmin,*' to my invocations," said the Prophet (ﷺ). The Prophet (ﷺ) then began to supplicate, and the butcher said '*Âmin,*' after each of his supplications. Suddenly a cloud appeared; rain fell from it into the nearby town, after which it approached the two men. Something strange then happened. Wherever the butcher walked, the cloud followed after him, instead of hovering over the Prophet (ﷺ).

"You claim that you have no good deeds," said the Prophet (ﷺ). "Yet, despite the fact that it was I who supplicated while you said, 'Âmin,' the cloud shaded the city, and then it followed you. What is your story?" The butcher then told him about what happened with his neighbor's daughter.

Now having a clear understanding of the butcher's situation, the Prophet (ﷺ) said, "One who repents to Allâh has a ranking that no other person can achieve."

---------- ❖ ❖ ❖ ----------

An Effective, Though Difficult, Way Of Fighting Off Temptation

Ibrâhim reported that a famous worshipper entered into a conversation with a woman. The conversation became more and more intimate, until the worshipper finally placed his hand on the woman's leg. Coming back to his senses, the worshipper removed his hand, left the woman, and placed his hand into fire, thus reminding himself of the unbearable Fire of the Hereafter.

---------- ❖ ❖ ❖ ----------

A Repentance That Involved Losing His Leg

The narrator of this story is Zaid bin Aslam:

Among the Children of Israel there once lived a man who devoted his life to worshiping Allâh (ﷻ) in his monastery. He stayed busy inside for a long time, until one day, he decided to look over the wall of his monastery to see what was going on outside. There near the wall stood a beautiful woman. Never having had such feelings before, the worshipper now desperately wanted to be with her and have her. He placed his leg through the window in order to go out to her, but no sooner did he manage to get one leg outside than Allâh (ﷻ) guided him back to his senses.

"What is it that I am trying to do?" he asked himself in astonishment. He felt a great deal of remorse for his evil intention, so much so that he refused to bring his leg inside again. "Never!" he exclaimed. "A leg that has gone outside to disobey Allâh (ﷻ) will never return with me to my monastery." He remained in the position he was in for a very long time, with his leg hanging outside. And throughout the various seasons of the year, that leg was subjected to fierce winds, to rain, to the sun, and to snow – until his leg became so wasted away that it had to be amputated. Such was the sincerity of his repentance.[1]

---

[1] A repentance that involves self-inflicting harm may have been acceptable in the laws that previous Prophets ﷺ came with, but it is certainly not acceptable in the *Shariah* of Muhammad (ﷺ). — *Editor*

The Repentance Of Barkh

It is reported that, during the era of Mûsa (🕮), the people were afflicted with a severe drought. They asked Mûsa (🕮) to go out and pray for rain.

"Come out with me to the mountain," Mûsa (🕮) said. When they were all together at the top of the mountain, Mûsa (🕮) said, "Let no man who has sinned follow me." More than half of the people left then. "Let no one who has sinned follow," repeated Mûsa (🕮). With the exception of a one-eyed man, whose name was Barkh Al-'Abid, everyone then parted.

"Did you not hear what I said?" asked Mûsa (🕮).

"Yes indeed," the man replied.

"And you have never perpetrated a sin?" asked Mûsa (🕮).

"I do not know if what I did is a sin unless I mention it (for you to judge). If it was really a sin, then I will leave."

"What did you do?" asked Mûsa (🕮).

"While I was walking on the road, I came across a home whose door was wide open. I stole a glance inside with my eye that is now missing, and I saw the form of some person. [Coming back to my senses (for it is unlawful to look into the home of another person)], I said to my eye,

'You are a part of my body, and you have hastened to commit a sin. You will no longer be a part of me!' I then dug my finger into my eye-socket and pulled my eye out. If what I did was a sin, then I will leave now."

"It was not a sin," said Mûsa (ﷺ). "Pray for rain, O Barkh." Honored by Mûsa's request, the man then began to pray for rain.

---------- ❖ ❖ ❖ ----------

A Repentant Journey
To The City Of The Righteous

It is reported that Ibn Mas'ûd (ﷺ) said, "There used to be two towns, one inhabited by righteous people and the other inhabited by wicked people. One of the male dwellers of the evil city once decided to go to the city of the righteous. (But he never completed his journey, for) the angel of death came to him where Allâh (ﷻ) willed (i.e., willed for the man to die). Once there, the angel (of Death) and the Devil got into a dispute. "By Allâh, he has never disobeyed me," said the Devil. "He came out (of the evil city) with the intention of repenting," answered the angel. In order for a judgment to be made between them, it was decided that a measurement should be made to see which of the two towns the man was closest to. They found that he was closer, albeit only by the span of a hand, to the city of the righteous. And so he was forgiven (for his sins)."

---------- ❖ ❖ ❖ ----------

The Thief Of The Children Of Israel

Wuhaib bin Al-Ward is the narrator of this story:

It has been conveyed to us that 'Îsa (﷽) and one of his disciples once passed by the tower of a thief. When the thief saw them, Allâh (﷽) guided him to repent. He said to himself: "This is 'Îsa (﷽)...the word of Allâh (i.e., Allâh said, "Be!" and he was), and this is one of his disciples. And who are you, O wretched one! You are the thief of the Children of Israel! You rob people on the road, you take their wealth, and you spill their blood!" He then descended to them, repentant for his past sins.

When he reached them, he said to himself: "Do you wish to walk alongside them? You are not worthy of that! Walk behind them, as is befitting of a sinner like you." The disciple turned around and, recognizing the thief, said to himself: "Look at this wicked, wretched person and how he walks behind us." Of course, Allâh (﷽) knew what was going on in the hearts of the thief and the disciple of 'Îsa (﷽): the former was feeling contrite and remorseful for his sins, while the latter was deriding him and deeming himself to be the superior of the two.

Allâh (﷽) then inspired to 'Îsâ bin Maryam (﷽) that he

should order both his disciple and the thief of the Children of Israel to begin their deeds anew (i.e., to begin with no past record of good or bad deeds). As for the thief, Allâh (﷾) forgave him on account of his contrition and repentance. And as for the disciple, all of his deeds became nullified on account of his being impressed with himself and of his derision of a person who repented [for his past sins (i.e., the former thief)].

---------- ❖ ❖ ❖ ----------

Be Pleased With Me

Mâlik Ar-Ruâsi reported that he, along with others from Banu Kilâb, attacked a group of people from the Banu Asad tribe. They killed some and dealt indecently with female prisoners. News of what happened reached the Prophet (ﷺ), who then cursed the attackers and supplicated against them.

When Mâlik heard about the Prophet's reaction to the attack, he tied his own hands, went to the Prophet (ﷺ), and said, "O Messenger of Allâh, be pleased with us (i.e., forgive us) – may Allâh be pleased with you."

The Prophet (ﷺ) turned away from him, but he went around the Prophet (ﷺ) to face him. He then repeated his previous plea: "Be pleased with us – may Allâh be pleased with you." He then said, "For by Allâh, when one tries to please the Lord (Allâh) (ﷻ), He becomes pleased (with him)." Drawing near to Mâlik, the Prophet (ﷺ) asked:

«تُبْتَ مِمَّا صَنَعْتَ أَسْتَغْفَرْتَ اللهَ؟»

"Have you repented for what you did? And have you asked Allâh to forgive you?"

"Yes," answered Mâlik.

«اللَّهُمَّ تُبْ عَلَيْهِ وَارْضَ عَنْهُ»

"O Allâh, pardon him and be pleased with him,"[1]

said the Prophet (ﷺ).

[1] *Usdul-Ghabah*: 4595

How To Ward Off
The Evils Of Wealth

Sa'id bin Ayman, the freed slave of Ka'b bin Sûr, said, "While the Messenger of Allâh (ﷺ) was speaking to his Companions (﷼), a poor man came and sat down beside a rich man. From his movement, it seemed as if the rich man were moving his garment away (so that the poor man wouldn't touch it). The Messenger of Allâh's (color) changed (from anger), and he (ﷺ) said:

«يَا فُلَانُ! أَخَشِيتَ أَنْ يَعْدُوَ غِنَاكَ عَلَيْهِ أَوْ أَنْ يَعْدُوَ فَقْرُهُ عَلَيْكَ؟»

'O so-and-so! Were you afraid that your richness would transfer to him, or that his poverty would transfer to you?'

'And is richness evil?' asked the (rich) man. The Prophet (ﷺ) said, 'Yes, for your richness invites you to the Hellfire, while his poverty invites him to Paradise.' The rich man asked, 'Then how can I save myself from that?' The Prophet (ﷺ) answered, 'Comfort him with some of it (i.e., with some of your wealth; meaning, give him charity).' The (rich) man said, 'I will do so then.' The poor man then spoke: 'I am in no need of it (i.e., of his charity).' The Prophet (ﷺ) said, 'Then ask (Allâh) to forgive your brother and supplicate for him.' "

A Complete Transformation

Ja'far bin Harb wasn't simply wealthy; he was also an important government figure, not officially, but he still enjoyed as much wealth and status as the Governors of the various provinces. In fact, when it came to important tasks, the ruler trusted Ja'far implicitly. Greatly preoccupied with worldly pursuits, Ja'far did not lend much of his time to apply the teachings of Islam. But then one day, he heard a man recite this Verse:

﴿أَلَمْ يَأْنِ لِلَّذِينَ ءَامَنُوٓاْ أَن تَخْشَعَ قُلُوبُهُمْ لِذِكْرِ ٱللَّهِ وَمَا نَزَلَ مِنَ ٱلْحَقِّ﴾

"Has not the time come for the hearts of those who believe (in the Oneness of Allâh – Islamic Monotheism) to be affected by Allâh's Reminder (this Qur'ân), and that which has been revealed of the truth."[1]

Ja'far called out: "O Allâh, yes...O Allâh, yes...O Allâh, yes (the time has indeed come for my heart to be affected by Allâh's Reminder)." He then cried many tears of sorrow for his former meaningless life.

He proceeded to distribute all of his wealth as atonement for his previous transgressions. When I say all of his wealth, I mean even his clothing. To cover his private areas, he walked into the shallow part of a river. Hearing about Ja'far's complete transformation, a man went to the river and gave him clothing as a gift. Now owning

---

[1] *Qur'ân* 57:16

nothing save the clothes he received as a gift, Ja'far dedicated the rest of his life to knowledge and worship.

The point of this and similar stories is not to encourage people to go to extremes in their lives; rather, it is to show how people from the earlier centuries of Islam underwent complete character transformations once they became guided to repenting from their sins. The questions we have to ask ourselves are these: Have we repented sincerely for our sins? If yes, then how much have we changed for the better? And how much more can we do to change for the better? And if no, then has not the time come for our hearts to be affected by Allâh's Reminder (the Qur'ân) and by what has been revealed of the truth?

---------- ❖ ❖ ❖ ----------

Giving Charity To Atone For Past Sins

Many of Al-Hasan Al-Basri's epigrammatic and wise sayings are still with us today. An eloquent speaker, Al-Hasan's sermons would penetrate the inner regions of his listeners' hearts. One day, a man named Habib bin Muhammad, who was mainly preoccupied in worldly pursuits, decided to attend Al-Hasan's gathering. While there, Habib became greatly moved by Al-Hasan's sermon, and when he left it, he decided to repent for his sins and to lead a new life of worship and obedience to Allâh (ﷺ).

The first order of business, decided Habib, was to purify his soul by giving charity. And he now had so much trust in Allâh (ﷺ), that he decided to give away a great deal of his wealth. He started off by giving away 10,000 dirhams in the early part of the day. Very soon thereafter, he gave away another 10,000 dirhams, after which he said, "(O my Lord,) this (10,000) is my gratitude for the guidance You have blessed me with." He then gave away another 10,000 dirhams, and this time he said, "O my Lord, if You did not accept from me the first amount or the second amount, then accept this from me." He then gave away yet another 10,000 dirhams, after which he said, "O my Lord! If you have accepted from me the third (amount), then this is a show of my gratitude (for You having accepted my deed)."

If You Have No Shame,
Then Do As You Please

One of the children of Al-Qa'nabi is the narrator of this story:

A regular drinker of wine, my father used to keep company with disreputable young men. He one day invited them and then sat down in front of his door, waiting for them to arrive. While he was waiting, Shu'bah passed by on his donkey, and a number of people were racing behind him in order to keep up with him.

"Who is that?" asked Al-Qa'nabi.

"Shu'bah," answered someone who was seated nearby.

"And what is a Sho'bah?" asked Al-Qa'nabi derisively.

"A scholar of *Hadîth*," was the reply. This explained why so many people were following Shu'bah, for they were probably his students. "Al-Qa'nabi, who was wearing an indecent, red-colored lower garment", said Al-Qa'nabi, in a peremptory and somewhat disdainful manner.

"You are not one of the people of *Hadîth*, so I do not feel obliged to relate a narration to you," said Shu'bah. Al-Qa'nabi, who had probably just imbibed a few drinks, took out a knife and pointed it menacingly at Shu'bah.

"You will report to me a narration or I will injure you," said Al-Qa'nabi.

"Mansûr reported to us," began As-Shu'bah, "From Rib'i

from Abu Mas'ûd, who said: The Messenger of Allâh (ﷺ) said:

«إِذَا لَمْ تَسْتَحِ فَاصْنَعْ مَا شِئْتَ»

'If you have no shame, then do as you please (one meaning of this narration might be: One who has no shame is one who does as he pleases, but he will certainly face the consequences of his actions).'[1]

Tossing the knife onto the ground, Al-Qa'nabi returned to the inside of his home. Not wanting the implications of the aforementioned *Hadîth* to apply to him, he took all of the wine bottles he had and emptied them onto the floor. He then said to his mother, "My companions will soon arrive. When they come, admit them inside and offer them food. When they are finished eating, tell them what I did with the alcohol, so that they will then leave." As for himself, Al-Qa'nabi immediately left for Al-Madinah, where he spent the following years of his life as a student of Imam Mâlik bin Anas – may Allâh have mercy on him. He eventually had the honor of reporting *Hadîth* narrations from the Imam.

---------- ❖ ❖ ❖ ----------

---
[1] *Al-Bukhari*: 6120

Give Charity, For Doing So Might Lead To Your Betterment

Abul-Hârith Al-Awlâsi once turned to a man and said, "Do you know how I first repented and mended my ways?"

"No," answered the man.

"When I was a young man, I was both handsome and energetic. But I was heedless of true guidance. Then one day, I saw a sick man lying down on the side of the road. I drew near to him and asked, 'Is there anything that you desire?' 'Yes,' he replied. 'A pomegranate.' I brought him what he asked for, and when I placed it in his hands, he looked up at me and said, 'May Allâh forgive you.' No sooner did the sun set on that day than did my heart undergo a complete transformation. Instead of being preoccupied with frivolous forms of entertainment, I suddenly became preoccupied with the fear of death."

---------- ❖ ❖ ❖ ----------

How To Reach One's Destination

Silah bin Ashyam used to spend his days worshiping near a graveyard; he probably chose that location so that he could see the graves from a distance and thus remember death and the Hereafter. Whenever he would walk to his designated place of worship, he would pass by a group of young men who would be wasting away the hours of the day in frivolous forms of entertainment. Silah used to stop and say to them, "Tell me – if a group of people intend to go on a journey, and if they spend their days playing on the road and their nights sleeping (in their tents), when will they reach their destination?" No doubt, the young men probably would have thought that he were crazy, had it not been for the fact that, in addition to those enigmatic words, he would admonish them and remind them about their religious duties.

One day, he passed by them and asked the same question that he always asked. One young man who was present in the group now understood Silah's words, and so turning to his companions, he said, "O people! By Allâh, he is referring particularly to us, for we play during the day and sleep during the night (i.e., so how will we reach Paradise)." He then followed Silah and, until he died, became his companion in worship – may Allâh have mercy on them both.

Which Of These Is More Beloved To Me?

Ibrâhim bin Al-Hârith is the narrator of this story:

There was once a man who was known for weeping from fear of Allâh (ﷻ). One day, when he was asked about his bouts of weeping, he said, "I cry when I remember the many ways in which I have wronged my own self, and when I remember how I have not been modest before He Who has the ability to punish me. He (ﷻ) has given me respite until the day of eternal punishment, the day of eternal misery. By Allâh, were I to be asked, 'Which is more desirable to you: for accountability to be taken of you and for you to then be ordered to be taken to Paradise, or for you to be dust,' I would choose to be dust."

---------- ❖ ❖ ❖ ----------

True Speech

Perhaps it was because he was righteous and they were not; perhaps they were jealous of him; whatever the reason, a group of people resented Rabi' bin Khuthaim, and so they decided to put him to trial. They chose the most beautiful woman they could find, and they offered her a reward of 1000 dirhams if she could successfully seduce him. After she agreed to take on the challenge, she attired herself in her most beautiful clothing and she put on the best perfume she could find.

Then she went to Rabi' and presented herself before him. They were all alone, and Rabi' seemed to be cornered; worse, her beautiful figure and face presented what seemed to be an inescapable temptation.

Approaching him, she moved her body enticingly and she spoke sweet, melodious words. What was Rabi' to do? He had nowhere to escape; her beauty had practically taken him as captive; and he had no weapon with which he could ward her off. But wait, he did have a weapon: the truth.

Addressing her with a resolute tone, Rabi' said, "What will you do if you are afflicted with disease and your body and beauty take a turn for the worse? What will you did when the angel of death comes to take your soul? Or what will you do when Munkar and Nakir test you in your grave?" He continued in this manner until the woman let out a shrill scream and fainted. When she regained consciousness, she repented for her past sins and, until the very end of her life, dedicated her days and nights to the worship of Allâh (ﷺ).

---------- ❖ ❖ ❖ ----------

Allâh's Vast And Comprehensive Mercy

Yûsuf bin Al-Husain is the narrator of this story:

I was with Dhi-an-Nûn on the edge of a stream, when we saw an extraordinarily large lizard crawling along the side of the stream. Something strange yet wonderful then happened. A frog surfaced from the stream, the lizard mounted its back, and the frog then swam to the other side of the stream, carrying its passenger on its back. Dhi-an-Nûn said, "There is something interesting about that lizard; let us go and follow it." We crossed the stream (which wasn't so wide in width), and on the other side, we saw a drunken man who had passed out. Suddenly, a snake appeared before the prone body of the drunkard. It slithered its way up the man's navel to his chest, making a direct course for one of his ears.

The lizard we saw earlier then sprang into action. It jumped onto the snake and struck it violently, splitting its body into two. Returning to the edge of the stream, the lizard then mounted the frog again, and the two crossed to the other side of the stream, though both were still visible to us. Dhi-an-Nûn woke up the drunkard, who slowly opened his eyes and became conscious of what was happening around him. Dhi-an-Nûn said, "O young man, look how Allâh has saved you! When this snake came to kill you, that lizard came and killed it." He then explained the entire story to the young man.

The young man stood up and exclaimed: "O my Lord, this is how You deal with one who disobeys You, then what will Your Mercy be like for the one who obeys You?" He then betook himself to the desert, vowing to dedicate his life to worship and to never return to the evils of the city.

---------- ❖ ❖ ❖ ----------